Sail into the Sunset

❋

A Handbook for 'Ancient Mariners'

Dedicated to all Sailing Octogenarians,
in the hope that we will live to join them

Sail into the Sunset

✳

A Handbook for 'Ancient Mariners'

BILL AND LAUREL COOPER

ADLARD COLES NAUTICAL
London

Published in 1994 by Adlard Coles Nautical
an imprint of A & C Black (Publishers) Ltd
35 Bedford Row, London WC1R 4JH

First edition 1994

ISBN 0-7136-3951-2

A CIP catalogue record for this book is available from the
British Library.

Typeset in 10^1/2 on 12pt Sabon by Falcon Graphic Art
Limited, Wallington
Printed and bound in Great Britain by The Cromwell Press,
Melksham, Wiltshire

CONTENTS

Lady Mayhew, doyenne of the lady one-design racers, sailing her Brown Boat, Pochard. At 93 she has only just given up active sailing, but is still the Chairman of the Broads One-Designs of the Royal Norfolk and Suffolk Yacht Club. Photo: Eastern Daily Press from The Brown Boats *by Charles Goodey.*

INTRODUCTION

THIS BOOK WAS written with *Hosanna* on the move from France via Corsica, Sardinia, Sicily, Italy, the Ionian Sea, the Aegean Sea, to Turkey, and back to Greece. We had no access to libraries, and only what reference books we carry, so apologies for factual errors. We wrote when sheltering from winter gales, in spells of rest after wild nights of anchor dragging, in peaceful anchorages and quiet bays, in good harbours and bad, with the company of other yachts and without. We were interrupted by the usual events of life at sea, change of wind or weather, failure of gear or gadgets, maintenance and mending, one or other of the ship's cats absent without leave, or falling in the water, necessitating rescue and dry towels, (will they never learn?) the welcome arrival of guests and the exchange of tales and views with other cruisers, some of them very ancient mariners indeed.

Our references and sea cred are based on our memories and experiences, and those of the people we met cruising, gallant old folk (no one in the book is younger than pensionable, and many are octogenarians), self-sufficient and content, and the observations are theirs as well as ours. Observations crystallize into opinions. Opinions are not fixed and immutable, nor are they sacred writ. Call them a point of view. The subject – what kind of boat to grow old in – is vast. It follows that there are apparent contradictions in the text, but if closely studied, it will be seen that a special case is being looked at, or a particular kind of boating. The perfect boat does not exist. If you find one adapted to your use that has few faults, you are doing better than most. If you fall in love with her, there is no more to say. Be content.

PART ONE

Dipping Your Toe in the Water

1

There is Life After Work

'You are old, Father William,' the young man said,
'And your hair has become very white,
And yet you incessantly go out in boats,
Do you think at your age it is right?'

'In my youth,' said the old man, 'I took to the sea,
I found it was good for me then,
And now, with the health and contentment it brings,
I shall live to a hundred and ten.'

WE ARE ALL, on average, living longer. We can expect two decades, even a quarter of a century of active life to follow our retirement. What shall we do with this precious time? Some of us, after a busy and satisfying working life, will sigh with contentment and turn to our gardens and our goldfish. Some of us may want to use our leftover life to catch up on things we have always wanted to do; hang-gliding perhaps, learning Sanskrit, or sailing across the Atlantic.

Many people want to retire to live in or around boats, and others might like to involve themselves in various different aspects of this water world, a world which fascinates as few others do. It is all of these people that we address, for while those who are used to boats may well be able to balance their capacities with their fancies and finances, those whose working lives have kept them from such nautical intimacy may feel the need of some guidance in general, and both groups may appreciate a collection of comments and experiences in order to achieve a suitable answer. This may not necessarily be the sensible one, since eccentricity is, thank God, still legal until fairly

*'Eccentricity is, thank God, still legal until fairly
advanced old age.'*

advanced old age. When it comes to a decision, access to informed points of view aside from your own predilections can help you to make up your mind.

Women are living longer than men these days. For countless generations the bothers of childbirth and the problems of ceasing to be bothered by them balanced the ills and accidents that male flesh was heir to, and ensured that on average, women and men had much the same prospect of mortality. When the medical profession removed many of the risks of breeding and sorted out some of the potential disasters of the menopause, added to the fact that women also tended to smoke less, women began to outlive their men. But that is not the whole of the story. Nowadays the probability of a *young* woman dying within any one year is much the same as for a man of the same age. The big differences in immediate mortality risks start to make themselves apparent round about the retirement age for men.

What a criminal squandering of resources our country tolerates, by having a fixed retirement age for people whose acquired knowledge, wisdom, commonsense, resourcefulness and dependability ought to be prized above rubies. The very fact that thousands of retired people take to the sea and make extraordinary voyages out of reach of social workers, completely capable and self-reliant until extreme old age, indicates the potential that is being lost. We need stimulation, modest adventure, stretching to our limits, exposure to new ideas. What use are the refurbished bodies that the doctors give us if our minds are allowed to stultify? We go to sea to keep our minds alive, and our bodies ticking over nicely. The more static souls choose to accomplish the same ends at home by gardening, cycling, walking the dog, and pursuing some beguiling obsession to stimulate the grey matter, railways perhaps, or mediaeval music. It is an insult beyond bearing that often all that is provided for these people in day centres and retirement homes is media pap and jigsaws. When we get very old we get patronised, nannied and grannied, and swept on to the scrapheap. The apathy that then afflicts us is imposed upon us by inactivity, and the will of our juniors. The lions are caged, and not enough of us roar.

There is a case for 'survival days out' for the elderly, as well as the young. Instead of a coach tour to Brighton and back, with everyone counted in and out, and a convenient loo every couple of hours, how much more rewarding (but difficult) it would be if the coach should deposit its charges in an unknown destination with a sum of money, and leave them to find out where they are, where the loo is, have lunch, and get back under their own steam. The stimulation provided would give a subject of chat for months, and would be worth a puddle or two on the restaurant floors.

And why cannot those of us dependent on our pensions get grants to achieve our life's ambitions, a sort of retraining grant for the last thirty years of our life? Not as a reward for industry, but as a sound economical proposition, since a contented population would cost far less in state medical bills and nursing home fees.

Nothing prolongs active life like work. It is quite apparent to us that retirement, a comparatively recent phenomenon, historically speaking, is a shock to the system from which many men never recover. They suffer seriously from loss of status, lack of aim, and boredom. Those who put up their metaphorical feet, and potter about getting in the way of their wives tend, even if they survive the murderous thoughts of their spouses, to die rather quickly.

Here, surely, is the clue to the differing life expectancies: women may retire from 'work', but go on cooking and housekeeping and gardening. While the men are suffering a sudden and traumatic change of life, the women keep blithely on, doing what they always did. Men who slide easily into retirement are those who can henceforth transfer their time and attention to passionate interests, and all who do this stand a better chance of living contentedly on to become a thorough nuisance to everyone and the despair of their pension fund trustees. It matters not what the interest is centred on: roses or riding, bridge or bowls, model railways or Monopoly, silk screen printing or sex for octogenarians, yoga or yachting. The important thing is to be obsessed almost, but not quite, to the point of mania.

Some of the happiest old people we know concern themselves with boats. Boats are not usually a part-time hobby. They move in on families, like rats in cold weather, they take over, and before you know it you are busier than you have ever been and, if willing, so is your partner. It takes up a lot of time and effort, and stops the neurons from atrophying. One's boat becomes the Neuron Protective Device. (Is it coincidence that an important part of the brain is the Hippocampus - the sea-horse?). In order not to go to the opposite extreme of overwork in the evening of one's days, one can choose a boat that will be easy to manage: one problem a day is probably enough to keep the grey cells functioning. Or if other interests figure in your plans you can do your yachting the lazy way, by chartering or flotilla holidays.

If you wish to do other things besides boating, things that require a land base for example, there is no need to be a gerontological world-girdler. (There are so many of these already: God forbid we should encourage many more.) There are those who stay at home and constitute the cylinder blocks of the nation's yacht clubs. For every dozen or so young sportsmen and women dashing about collecting the silverware and getting all the publicity, there are as many dozens of loyal hard-working folk in the background making it easy for the champions. The trophy-hunters become the surrogate young of their elders and give much vicarious pleasure by their achievements.

Happiness at sea after long years of work depends on your aim, your ability, and your attitude. If you are clear about your aim, go for it. Look at your abilities with merciless detachment and see if you can improve them if need be, since they will affect the aim. If you cannot alter your abilities you may have to modify your aim. Attitude can greatly affect your future life and is the subtlest and least susceptible to change. Some people are born miserable, live miserable, and cannot expect a happy retirement. The happy ones, we observe, are not those with most money and possessions, but those with open minds, moderate expectations, and a pleasantly busy life. Of these endowments, an attitude of moderate expectation becomes more important with age. Nothing is perfect, as the Philosopher said of the porridge; there are lumps in it. Ask not why the rose bush should bear thorns: rather be glad the thorn bush bears roses.

As we grow older, both of us find we must moderate our expectations even more, not as regards the wide world outside, which we still find wonderful and exciting, if flawed; but in what we expect of ourselves. This expectation is at present undergoing modification. Exasperating as it may be, it is becoming easier to keep our minds flexible than our knees, our physical work spells shorten with our breath and our temper, a long siesta in the hot part of the day has become annoyingly desirable. If we are not to fall out with our bodies, we are going to have to make fewer demands on them, and treat them with a little more loving care than was our wont. This does not mix well with a Protestant work ethic. That, too, will have to be modified.

It is our intention in this book to discuss the various ways in which a person contemplating retirement can involve him or herself in yachting. We use the word yachting here because it has a precise definition: activity in boats for the purpose of pleasure. (The *Shorter Oxford Dictionary*, thinking of Charles the Second, and very possibly not revised since he was on the throne, describes a yacht as a light fast sailing ship for the conveyance of royal or other important persons. Not in our book, it isn't.)

We shall look at the aspects of yachting that we think might be of interest to a person contemplating retirement, whether it is early retirement which seems to be happening more in these days of recession, or the normal retirement at 60 or so. We once had as our motto: 'retire early - retire often', our version of a philosophy held by the writer John D MacDonald's fictional boat-bum Travis McGee; though the idea of taking your retirement in instalments throughout life is becoming harder to realise as job opportunities decline.

Many will already have some experience of yachting in one or other of its several forms. Perhaps they will simply continue their activities with minor adjustments in emphasis compatible with decreasing physical ability. In the mind of the person who has always had a call for things nautical but has never been able to spare the time to acquire skill or experience we hope to sow the seeds of a flourishing and successful new life. Some of the groundwork is in *Sell Up and Sail,* and we do not wish to repeat tiresomely what we said there. This book is the fine tuning for what we refuse to call your declining years. There is a long section on different kinds of boat, and some thoughts on their uses, as well as a 'watch out' section under the heading of 'Don't Shoot the Albatross' (you will remember that the Ancient Mariner's troubles began when he shot the bird of good omen with his crossbow).

When you were young, you were probably pushed about by your elders; while you were at work you were ruled by your contemporaries, but now, quick, in the period before you will be pushed about by your offspring or the Welfare Machine, you can do what you wish. For this gloriously golden spell in your lives, you are master of your destiny, and have the maturity to enjoy it to the full.

2

Ancient Mariners

Sailor boy Blue
You've rounded the Horn
Your gallant red duster
Is tattered and torn
Where's the old boy who looks after the ship?
Down at the pub, celebrating his trip.

WE DO NOT KNOW any centenarians who still race yachts, though we are prepared to believe there are some, somewhere. We have known two stalwarts, one a woman, who went on actively racing well into their eighties. Both were East Anglians, it is true; they are notoriously long-lived out there where the east wind blows the hair off your head, but cannot freeze your innards, since they are well insulated with suet pudding, our natural regional diet.

Mr Clabburn went on racing his Yare and Bure One-Design for as long as anyone could remember, always wearing the same yellow pullover, and watched by what appeared, year in and year out, to be the same black labrador, his greatest fan, who would count the three rounds of the race from the waterside lawn in front of the clubhouse and then amble down to the jetty to welcome his master in. The only occasion when he failed in this rendezvous was when the race was shortened due to lack of wind; the dog was not programmed for this. It seemed he could count three but not two.

Lady Mayhew sailed her Broads One Design off Lowestoft at an age when her venerable locks could have won her a fireside chair and a knitted shawl. Sharp as mustard, you might say (she was a Colman), she personified the class for almost a lifetime.

While Mr Clabburn raced entirely on inland waters, the Lady was ever willing to get the salt spray in her hair, which is virtually unavoidable in the rough waters off Lowestoft, and get her feet wet, equally inevitable given that the Brown Boats, as they were called, were well known for being as wet as they were brown.

Many other people in the October of their days were active in a variety of ways in the yacht clubs where we cut our nautical teeth. All of them were characters, some of them bad.

Among the good, Gerald Sambrooke Sturgess was the leading authority in the country, not to say the world, for his encyclopaedic knowledge of the yacht racing rules, which got steadily more complex with case law until one almost needed to brief counsel to decide race protests. His name was a byword for settling disputes between rival yachts.

Doctor Tracey was the doyen of the Norfolk Punt Club, a charming man, always helpful to youngsters. At that time the punts were the fastest small racing boats afloat, and he may have been the speediest ancient mariner of his days.

'Daddy' Bickmore roared his way about the Broads in his cruising yacht, aptly named *Rogue*, dedicated to educating the incompetent at the top of his not inconsiderable voice, while Doctor and Mrs Tidcombe spent their weekends as regular and reliable timekeepers on the finishing line at all the Wroxham regattas.

Sidney Mobbs enriched his latter days by puttering round Oulton Broad in his launch *Petagin*, which we owned for a while after him. He liked shouting at the hire boats, but he also enjoyed getting in the way of yacht races, and would go happily home to his tea refreshed by a day in the fresh air, rounded off by a really good shouting match to give him an appetite.

Bob Applegate was ancient when he taught Laurel's father to sail. The block that took the halyard at the top of the mast squeaked horribly. 'Do yew know what that there block say to me?' he asked, pointing upwards with a forefinger bright brown with nicotine. 'That say *Can't afford it! Can't afford it!*'

We do not apologise because these are all East Anglians: that is our native land, and clearly they are the people we know best. You would be able to find a similar list anywhere, and might have fun compiling one.

All these people had a busy and rewarding old age. But they were not themselves exceptional. They gave time and effort to what they found enjoyment in doing, and all of them found a rich vein of contentment.

Others we know of have gone happily off to sea.

Ancient mariners all
Countless people in most of the seas of the world are successfully sailing into their eighties. They look fit and happy. Are they fit and happy

because they are sailing, or are they sailing because they are fit and happy? Which is the chicken and which is the egg?

We think we can do no better than to quote the examples of some well-known sailors who were of an age that most would accept as senior. These people went on doing things, or even started doing things that put most youngsters into the background even when considered on level terms.

Take Bill Tilman, born in 1898, who went on skippering his various very uncomfortable boats on expeditions to the Arctic and Antarctic, climbing there the sort of mountains that make experienced mountaineers gasp. He was, when he recently died on active service, of an age unimaginable, as a French admirer put it.

Francis Chichester was 65 when he made the singlehanded circumnavigation that earned his knighthood, and we think we are right in saying that he made the journey against his doctor's advice.

Sir Alec Rose was 60 when he followed shortly after on the same route, with a lifelong ambition but comparatively little deep sea experience.

Humphrey Barton, one of the founders of the Ocean Cruising Club, went on sailing into his old age, all over the place, almost to the despair of his family. But to their credit they let him do so, for it was what he wanted to do, and what he was still just about capable of doing.

Admiral Sir Lennon Goldsmith was still cruising singlehanded about the Aegean, which is by no means an easy cruising ground, dominated as it is in summer by the potentially violent *meltemi* wind, until well into his 80s.

George Fairley went on sailing his little 27 footer round and round the world singlehanded when any social worker would have made him swallow the anchor and hauled him ashore into care. He had diabetes that he could barely control, but he was as contented as his illness allowed him to be. So far as we know he never had to ask for help at sea, though he occasionally needed it in harbour.

Colonel Blondie Hasler was a mere chicken of 50 when he sailed his little junk-rigged folkboat *Jester* in the first Singlehanded Transatlantic race, and was still competing many years later. (His boat went on sailing, being inherited by another ancient mariner, Michael Richey, retired Secretary of the Royal Institute of Navigation, who is also still competing, even though *Jester* is no more.)

Captain Henry Denham cruised the Greek seas and eastern Med into his 80s, and wrote what are still the best yachting guides (as opposed to pilot books) of the area. He has just died, aged 92.

The Hiscocks, Eric and Susan, at 60, with two circumnavigations under their belts, built *Wanderer IV* and set out for the Pacific and

New Zealand. It seemed at one time that they would never stop. Their books on their voyages are classics, and were probably the original inspiration of us all.

And they are not all British, these senior sailors. Remember Don Street who writes and cruises in Iolaire, a boat almost as old as he is (or is it the other way round?) And Eric Tabarly, the brilliant French sailor - he is no chicken. Or Arthur Beiser, the American writer, who still cruises long distances every summer.

Do we need to go on? There are thousands more whose names would mean little to the public because they are unpublished, and unsung, but have completed without fuss stunning voyages at ages which most people associate with pipe and slippers, and knitting by the fire.

Bill, who has been at sea in one way or another for half a century, observed many years ago that he would rather have as crew in bad conditions a 70-year old who was wise, than an athletic youngster who thought he knew it all. He has only changed that point of view in the meantime to delete the word 'bad' before 'conditions', and substitute 'all', and to add 'of either sex' after '70-year old'.

One or two people with whom we have discussed the project to write this book have expressed doubts about the wisdom of encouraging older people to do what some worthy and caring folk think they are completely incapable of achieving, ie long distance cruising.

Most of the worriers dealt, in actuality, with extremely old people who could no longer look after themselves. We felt they were out of touch with the very large number who can cope perfectly well, and who can make their own decisions with intelligence and the wisdom that comes from long experience of life. In particular we feel that we are (to some extent) addressing those for whom real old age is still ahead; they may be knocking at the door, but they have not yet crossed the threshold, and have no desire to do so until they have exhausted the pleasures on this side. There is usually no coming back.

We cannot leave the subject without saluting some mariners who are not merely ancient, but have handicaps as well. Tristan Jones makes mighty voyages with one leg, and John Flewitt with none at all. If the will is there, ways can be found.

Single-handed sailing

We have had many discussions with people contemplating solo voyaging as a solace for their widow(er)hood. We have usually urged caution in approaching what must seem to be an obvious solution.

Wandering about the world we have met many solo voyagers, and observe that when we do meet them they never stop talking. Like the original Ancient Mariner, they hold you with a glittering eye, and you cannot choose but hear. Their volubility is natural if they have not seen a soul for weeks, but it suggests that even solo sailors need more or less regular doses of company. Of course there have been serene and happy soloists who lack nothing, and drop in and out of the busy world with ease. These have gone on well into old age, and then died content, thus attracting some attention. Little notice is taken of those for whom the experience was less than fascinating, unless it ends in disaster. The population of long-distance solo yachtsmen undoubtedly includes a number who have clearly gone round the bend, become anti-social, difficult to get on with, and even paranoic. It has to be said that some soloists are at sea on their own because nobody in their right mind would go with them.

One we met in the West Indies is stamped indelibly on our memory. We were talking about weapons, and said that we carried none. 'I've got my old Naval sword', said this singlehander, and told us the following story.

'I was moored to a wooden quay in X (he named a central American state), tired after a long passage. I heard splashing, and dashed topside to see a man climbing out of the sea and on to the end of the quay. He approached me and asked for cigarettes.'

'What did you do then?' we asked.

'I killed him, of course. A yard of cold steel straight through the heart.'

The phrase has engraved itself in our minds. Bystanders are sometimes shaken to hear one of us say, in reply to the question: what did you do then?

'I killed him, of course.'

Other singlehanders have been so sane and content and a pleasure to know that even though they are a small sample, their situations are worth considering because they appear to have solved their problem successfully.

One of the keys to success is familiarity. Those who have started singlehanding early become adapted to, and accept, its disadvantages. They are better able to enjoy the good times and have the resources to override the bad. But even those who adapt show some odd traits when, as they inevitably do, they find themselves in a social setting. All ancient mariners are a little odd, but the singlehanders, with no one else to answer to, or curb their habits, tend to become even odder, and fixed in their ways, as old maids used to be thought to do. Man is a fundamentally sociable animal, and the life of a sea hermit needs careful adaptation and should be contemplated only by those of a suitable temperament.

Even more caution is necessary for anyone widowed in their late maturity, especially after a good marriage. Many years of shared joys and sorrows cannot be lightly worked off. We feel there is ample evidence that too much solitude after grief is likely to lead to depression. Widow(er)s would need to be sure that the grieving had been fully worked through and life adjusted to new outlooks and perspectives before cutting themselves off as effectively as the solitary boat-dweller can, and often does.

What needs to be considered is the fact that if things go wrong, you are on your own. Two crocks are usually better than one, each complementing the other and giving encouragement; one can rest while the other keeps watch.

That said, we leave it to you. Solitude is not necessarily loneliness, and some sailors are admirably suited to it. It is perhaps the ultimate voyage, just you and your boat. You alone solve the problems and achieve the aim. There is the added luxury of having no one else to consider, so you can do what you please, when you please. You can eat what you like, when you like. You can turn the radio up, down or off, read with your elbows on the table, pick your nose with impunity, and cut your toenails all over the cabin sole. You can keep hens in a cage, a dozen cats, or play the bagpipes (all these instances are true). No point being old if you can't be a bit eccentric.

Cruising by crewing

Another way of sailing for singles is to crew for others. On our journeys we have met widows or widowers (and one bachelor, too, it must be said) who lead very active and contented lives involving the sea without regular partners. We have not met so many of these as we have the solo wanderer, perhaps because more follow the romantic solo path.

Though every case is different, and people go about their enjoyments and sorrows in differing ways, there are common features to the crewing option, and an example might distil the essence.

Consider a woman who was widowed while still very active. She was used to sailing with her husband, but did not feel competent to skipper a boat on her own. She did not wish to remain solitary, but was wary of the potential hazards of choosing a companion from the personal columns of the yachting magazines. In any event, she was not committed to spending her entire life yachting, and had some other healthy interests.

She became a paid hand on charter yachts skippered by people already known to her, and enjoyed the work immensely. She also crewed yacht deliveries, which tends to be a punishing way of life, but she remained cheerful and undaunted, and perfected her craft. Sometimes she maintained and looked after a boat for the winter, seeing to the varnish and paintwork and checking the engine and batteries.

Nowadays she crews for friends wanting an extra hand on an ocean crossing, or a tricky passage, and passes most of her summers this way. She has her own gear, she can hand, reef and steer. She expects her keep while on board, but will pay her own fares before or after the voyage. She is capable, tactful, good company, and best of all reliable, all the things a normal yachtsman could reasonably demand of his crew.

Now she is a pensioner she seems to spend more time afloat than ashore. She has made several trips with us, including one Atlantic crossing, and was an excellent crew, not hanging back in the bad weather. She was up there on the foredeck up to her waist in sea water shifting headsails in a squall. She never argued, and once she had got her breath back she had a fund of stories to help pass the time. This woman has more ocean crossings in her log than almost any younger salty dog you care to name. She manages to keep her multitude of skippers in order (most of whom reserve her services well in advance, and time after time) by threatening to write a book about the eccentric ones she has known. She will call it *Here We Go Gathering Nuts At Sea*. We all live in fear of its publication, but she is so good natured that we are sure she will hurt no one. Are you there, Betty?

Betty's personal panic bag

This is well worth recording here. As she says, you may not know what the skipper will provide, and there are certain things she does not wish to do without. You learn, she says, that a pack of novice youngsters can never find their own safety harnesses, and take yours when they dash up on watch. Worse, they readjust it to a 30 inch chest, so that when she does get it back she cannot get it on in a hurry. Hers is now integral to her hard weather jacket. The small bag that would accompany her into a liferaft contains:

- One miniature folding umbrella (to be used for shade, or upside down for catching a shower of rain)
- A small plastic bottle to tip the water into
- A small handbearing compass
- A seaman's claspknife
- A mirror
- A small torch with spare battery in waterproof wrapping
- Horlicks tablets and barley sugar
- Wet wipes
- Fish hooks and line
- Dark sunglasses and a cotton sunhat
- A hank of tarred string
- Lipsalve

Yachting is not all glamour. Here we see what the well-dressed Society Yachtswoman was wearing last spring.

- A mini toothbrush
- A change of underwear

At our suggestion she added:

- A bottle of multivitamin tablets
- A space blanket (folds into matchbox size)
- Total sunscreen

Betty is never seasick, but most people would add whatever brand of pill suits them best. All this packs into an astonishingly small space.

Now that insurers are demanding that a third hand is taken on long passages, there is a demand to be met. It is far better to take someone known, trusted and recommended than rely on picking up possibly dubious characters at the last minute. The only time we were forced into taking crew by our insurers we were plagued with incompetence and (ironically) petty theft, but worse has happened to others; a temporary crew once hijacked an entire boat in mid-Atlantic.

One can understand the popularity of reliable crew. Also that of an elderly man who has made a name as a sea-cook on long voyages and on ocean races. He is never sea-sick, does not do any of the on-deck work, but is so efficient at what he does that he is heavily in demand, and a well liked member of any crew. One owner who sailed with an all-male crew reported that he turned belowdecks from a slum to an elegant home.

A word of caution is necessary about the possibilities of engaging oneself as crew for longish voyages. It is necessary to have some reliable reference that the skipper is competent. Mere ownership of a nice-looking yacht and a suave manner are not adequate. We know of Atlantic crossings, and long deliveries to the Far East, planned by people who should never have been allowed to be in a boat at all, let alone advertise for crew. The RYA Offshore Yachtmaster's Certificate is the least you should require from someone you do not know; it is not a guarantee, but it is a good indicator, and better in this respect than a full Master Mariner's ticket, the holder of which may never have been in a craft under 30 000 tons. It is necessary to form some opinion as to the skipper's likely response to stress, and also to ascertain the prospective programme for the yacht. For example, someone with the idea of going from Colombo to Britain with planned stops only in Jeddah and Algiers, and starting off into the middle of the south-west monsoon needs to be given a wide berth. Anyone planning to do anything the 'hard way' should be left to suffer on their own, unless they can find fellow-masochists to suffer with them.

There is no need for crewing to be so actively ambitious if you do not wish. Large numbers of people occupy themselves and keep their social contacts by crewing in the rallies of various local cruising clubs, or by serving in various capacities in our yacht clubs. Some of them fill in as spare crew for a race or a day sail, and either way they can be invaluable.

One of the great things in life is to be valued. How nice to share a night watch or a dinghy race with people who respect you, to be part of a team, and to be pleasant and cheerful company, sought even by the young!

We could not end this little survey of what senior yachtsmen and women are doing without a brief mention of the numbers of couples sailing all waters with each other only. It seems there are so many who can achieve perfect happiness from this very peaceful pursuit, which can be undertaken with various degrees of energy so that it is continuable into very old age and very low ability. Those who want no heroics, and no dangers and derring-do, may look out on the world with modest expectations and be content. Ancient Mariners in their wide variety of craft regard each other with no appreciable snobbery, not of class, nor achievement, nor professionalism. Best of all, their age does not segregate them out of the mainstream, and they rub fenders with sailors of all ages. At this level all are sharing one of life's greatest pleasures: mucking about in boats.

3

Club Sailing

There was a little man, and he had a starting gun,
And he fired it to start off a race, race, race,
One yacht got too near, and before she could get clear
Her spinnaker was blasted into lace, lace, lace.

IT IS ALL VERY WELL being obsessed with boats and water, as we suppose we are, but there are many who would like some involvement
without going overboard, either actually or metaphorically. A bit of
fun or quiet pleasure during the warmer season, close to home, and
without spending too much money or energy. Perhaps only one half of
the team is really interested.

There is much activity varying from the obsessional to the casual
centred round local yacht clubs, both the grand and prestigious with
their frequent social functions, and the quasi backyard affairs consist-
ing of impecunious enthusiasts, and all stations between.

Joining the club
If your desire is to be involved in boats in your local area, particularly
if you want to cruise in company, or race, then you might well want to
join a local club. If there is more than one and their aims and facilities
are very different, it is worth doing a little research to find out which
will best suit your aim, and whether they will have you. This can be
almost insurmountably difficult if you are new to the area and have
previously had nothing to do with boats, a fact which would astonish
most clubs who like to feel that they are approachable and user
friendly. So most of them are if you have a track record. But if you
have not, and no friend to introduce you, then you must be bold, get
the address from the library, and ring or write to the Club Secretary.
Of course not all clubs want new members, and anyway you would

17

need proposers and seconders who could vouch for the fact that you are a splendid fellow who will not burgle the trophy cupboard or make off with the Ladies' Race tea fund (or even the ladies themselves), but there are clubs actively expanding their membership. If the membership is full the Secretary will say so, and if it is not you should get an answer to your questions. A probationary membership usually solves the proposer and seconder problem if the club is seeking new members.

The cost of subscriptions to yacht clubs is as variable as the difficulty of joining them. The annual subscription to some clubs is really very small. Sometimes it is only a few pounds, and these are often the friendliest. In these circumstances there is usually no grand clubhouse, and facilities can be a bit primitive. Other clubs' subscriptions could run to over two hundred guineas, plus a healthy entrance fee. This latter usually indicates a club with property: the property belongs to the members, and a new member is expected to pay something towards diluting the value of the existing members' assets. Clubs with high subscriptions are not necessarily snobbish. They can be, but it usually indicates that they offer extensive social and other facilities and have to employ staff to maintain their services.

There are some clubs that are prepared to compound their subscriptions with a commitment to do actual work for the club, and most clubs have a reduced subscription for older, long-service members. Details vary considerably.

Admin

If this is the field you are interested in, you do not even need a boat. In fact, it could be a drawback, since caring for boats can occupy large chunks of your time.

In all except the most prestigious and expensive clubs the full-time paid officials such as club secretaries have ceased to exist. This is not merely because there are nowadays fewer retired Majors and Lieutenant-Commanders wishing to eke out the meagre pension granted by an ungrateful nation, but it is also due to clubs being less flush with money. Thus there are many clubs who are delighted to find persons with administrative skills who are willing to help out. Usually expenses are paid, and often a small honorarium.

The opportunities are generally self-evident. Retired accountants and actuaries can help as Hon Treasurers, there is often work for Hon Solicitors if the club has property, those experienced in building or engineering are often in demand, and the computer literate are very welcome. People who are obsessed with racing, for instance, often have little time to devote to the running of the clubs on which their enjoyment of the sport depends.

There is no clearing-house for such talent. Posts are not advertised; very often the candidate creates his own post bit by bit and becomes indispensable with time. Generally things start by meeting members and talking to the club's officers, for there are few clubs that do not have the occasional crisis finding somebody to take over from George who has just had to give it up. People who are prepared to dedicate themselves are becoming rare, and this is an area where a retired person who is interested in the sailing ambience but is happy to watch from the shore can contribute a great deal. The Little Ship Club, for instance has recently lost a most treasured Secretary, the widow of a retired naval officer, who came to the job almost by accident but who ended up so nearly indispensable that her untimely death has thrown the club into noticeable (temporary, we hope) disorder.

It is becoming wise for yacht clubs to find somebody retired to take on these tasks. Younger people are much more mobile in their work these days and do not stay in the same job, or even locality, indefinitely. A club can be badly thrown if two bright young officers change their jobs and move out of the area at the same time. The retired generally have a certain stasis, and do not tend to go off and live somewhere else at a moment's notice; thus on a committee they can form a steady framework that complements the talents of the peripatetic young. Do not let anyone say that energy and initiative are the monopoly of the young. We'll poke their eyes out with our walking sticks.

Clearly the retired person even of impeccable qualification and excellence cannot expect to walk straight into a position of command and authority. There is much pleasure to be gained joining in at a humble level; wisdom and ability soon make an impression. There is something endearing about the retired managing director of a major property company up to his knees in cement helping to build a slipway. Surprising how much he enjoys it. A retired headmistress would probably find it even more fun.

Competitive spirits: club racing

Suppose the passive or administrative side of yachting does not appeal to you, and you feel you would like to take a more strenuously active part on the racing side. The best way of finding out what is going on is to do some racing yourself, as crew. Unless you are already skilled, in which case there is little we can tell you, there will be faint prospect of participating in the international red-hot classes of boat. Not only do these classes usually need a certain athleticism which you may not be able to look forward to retaining indefinitely even if you still have it, but they also harbour the whizz-kids, the pundits, the champions and the would-be champions, often enjoying open or tacit sponsorship. These conditions make it hard for a newcomer to break in, and do not lead to good racing for the less expert. Like ballet dancing, you should have begun aged eight, in order to continue doing it at 50. Bob Koch can skipper the America's Cup winner aged 60 plus because he has an unfair advantage: he is extremely rich. Even though there ought to be as much fun in racing to avoid being last as the champions find in striving for the winning gun, it palls after a time if you are always getting in half an hour after the rest of the fleet, who have drunk all the cold beer.

That said, there are plenty of examples of older people holding their own among the crack fleets. There were septuagenarians in the world Laser class championships this year, and they didn't ask for or get any concessions from the young in achieving very respectable results. This is a good class to consider, there is an enormous number of boats, they are found in many locations, and everyone says they are fun to sail.

Is there anywhere, in any class, a world championship for the older sailor? Would anyone (the French, perhaps, they are very good at this sort of thing) like to organise or sponsor a world championship *pour les marins de l'age d'or*?

If you moderate your expectations you can race with a club one-design class, or in the menagerie races which cater for all boats on a handicap basis. Many of the one-design classes are very old, and so are some of their skippers. Do not underrate them, they are wily old birds, worth crewing for and learning from. The more irascible of them sometimes have trouble finding crew, there's your chance, but don't say we said so. The Yare and Bure One-Designs (known as the White Boats) mentioned earlier first appeared on the scene at about the turn of the last century, and we had boat number 3, *Purple Emperor*, in our family for a time. (All the boats are named after butterflies.) Laurel's mother Linet sailed this in her 60s with great panache but not much skill, bouncing off other boats in a high wind with laughing apology. She did not excuse such collisions in others, particularly motor-driven hire craft, which tended to bring out the fishwife in her. Her husband Felix, a cautious man, sailed with quiet competence but no panache at all. He had learnt to sail in Great Uncle Arthur's halfdecker, a boat very like *Purple Emperor*. Laurel's Great Uncle Arthur was the Terror of the Broads at the turn of the century. He sailed rather worse than Linet, but never apologised, laughingly or otherwise, and shouted at Great Aunt Alice whenever he made a particularly glaring and expensive error. For minor dramas such as going

'The Terror of the Broads...'

aground or fetching up in the reeds he shouted at the maid whom they always took with them to mind the picnic basket.

The White Boats come to our mind because being old-fashioned they are simply rigged, spacious, moderately stable and quite comfortable to sit in. Modern yachts may be state-of-the-art, but it is hard to find one that is sufficiently uncluttered by gadgets to put both feet down together, or find a space for your handbag, still less your walking stick. The smaller boats can be unkind to old bones; they tip and bounce like a ping-pong ball in a millrace. The White Boats have been modernised in so far as the newer boats are now made of glassfibre from a mould off one of the old wooden hulls, which makes for easy maintenance. Many other clubs have boats, generally about twenty feet in length, with similar friendly characteristics.

To find out more about the clubs offering one-design racing in Britain you could consult the Royal Yachting Association, preferably at their stand at the Boat Show in London in early January. Go to the stand twice and consult different people each time. All yachtsmen are opinionated, even us, and you do not want to risk getting only one side of a story. (You may end up, as we did when we tested this advice, by being given copies of completely inappropriate leaflets by someone clearly looking forward to their lunch-break. That is just the luck of the draw, you will have to go three times.)

The RYA also has a leaflet which, among the lists of yacht club secretaries' addresses, gives the addresses of the secretaries of most of the racing classes. It doesn't describe the classes. (No one is going to do that much research for you.) You should then watch out for information in the yachting journals that report on club racing, such as *Yachts and Yachting*. It is true these tend to concentrate on international and national classes, but in fact there are one-designs in these categories that are raced locally in less than grand prix conditions. In addition most clubs offer racing in all types and one can get a good idea of the kind of club from the reports of the racing.

One-designs we have known (apart from our own East Anglian classes) include the Victory and X classes on the Solent, the Royal Burnham One-Design and the 'Tee-ods' from the Thames Estuary (not considered to be *really* East Coast), and the Yorkshire One-Design. Others we have heard about, but not actually sailed, are based at Falmouth, Dublin, Belfast, the Clyde, and at many places in Scotland. There are international one-design classes too, but because there is less strict control over the building they often have some of the characteristics of restricted classes in which alterations are allowed, thus increasing the expense. Examples are the Dragon and the Star, both exciting boats that are inclined to leave one a little wet at the end of a good sail, and a little short in the pocket at the end of the season.

There are some One-Design dinghy classes: the Dart and the Norfolk, both of which are traditional long reputation designs, the Sharpies and Snipes. There are many more local examples round our coasts that form the real base of local sailing, far too many for us to have personal knowledge of them all. Many have been in existence for decades, not an inappropriate quality for our readers.

This type of club One-Design racing at levels below that of international competition is not found in all yachting countries. Former British colonies indulge; we remember racing this way at Karachi, Colombo, Sandakan, Jesselton, Hong Kong, Singapore, and Bermuda. We know there is plenty in Australia and New Zealand, and recall good times at Watch Hill in Rhode Island, USA, while good class racing exists on the west coast of America, and in the Great Lakes, too.

Decide, too, if you want to go to sea or have a gentler sail on calm waters. Races off the coast tend to be cancelled more often; conditions are more rugged, they require more elaborate rigging and equipment, and the safety requirements are more demanding, which makes the boats a bit more expensive. You would also need better foulweather

'Better foulweather gear than wellies and a plastic mac ...'

gear than wellies and a plastic mac, and the serious yachting gear is now very expensive indeed. In any event if you are a novice you will need to acquire basic skills and improve on them before being able to get much satisfaction in racing, however informal and friendly.

You can acquire these skills at a sailing school. Many of these are represented at boat shows. Ask them some pre-considered questions, and if you cannot understand the answers you are clearly talking to the wrong kind of teachers. Learn the rudiments, and then offer yourself as crew to another, more experienced helmsman. Willing and reliable crews are hard to find, and this could be the key to your welcome into the sport. Generally speaking, sailing is one of the subjects that cannot be taught: it has to be learned, though it is valuable to be pointed in the right direction.

Cruising clubs

If you decide on a more relaxed approach to boating there are many clubs that cater for the cruising yachtsman. Some are local, and will cruise in company over a limited area, sometimes on inland waters. Others are for those who would like to cruise on their own for longer distances, even world-wide. We will discuss cruising as such later on, but now would be the time to talk about the cruising clubs.

Many of these are really loose associations of like-minded people who are held together by a periodical newsletter which disseminates information, and by out-of-season social and educational activities. Many of them have libraries of reference books and charts for members to consult, very interesting lectures, and a noticeably chummy feeling that can be lacking in some of the more 'professional' racing clubs.

These reference libraries need willing helpers, lecture programmes need arranging, articles for the magazine need writing, sifting, and processing, and because the membership of these clubs is widespread there is often more secretarial work to be done. Since the active membership is often away cruising, many of these clubs welcome part-time assistance.

Unfortunately some of them are hard to join. To qualify for the Ocean Cruising Club, for example, you must have accomplished a very long ocean voyage (1000 miles, port to port in a small yacht), and this is a club that has found administration something of a nightmare in the past. Evidently long-distance sailors are anarchists or are out of reach of the post office (from personal experience both of these conditions are valid). The Little Ship Club is actively seeking new members at present, now that it has settled into its superb new

Thameside quarters, courtesy of a Japanese property company who bought their old freehold. Other such clubs are the Cruising Association, based in London, and several Forces-oriented clubs. Many such clubs would welcome assistance from willing parties, whether or not they were formally qualified for membership. (Rules can be modified if the end result is desirable.) The technique is to start out as an informal helper, supposing that you live near one of the officers, and are known to him, and then make yourself indispensable. It doesn't take long, though it takes a little skill. For anyone with a vicarious interest in travelling, this sort of correspondence job could be very rewarding. It amounts to worldwide penfriendship, and could suit someone who is housebound, for example.

One of the facilities most craved by long-distance cruising yachtsmen is a mail-forwarding service. This could be a very interesting pastime for a disabled person, though as we discuss further on, there are not many disabilities that stop you cruising. Age does not count as a disability.

Clubs are not so popular in European countries, except for the Netherlands, which has similar clubs to those found in Britain and the USA. In the Mediterranean, yacht clubs are usually commercial affairs, though there are some in France and Italy that would be recognisable to Britons or Americans.

Clubs for those interested in the Inland Waterways enable you to help to restore or keep open navigation on some of Britain's old canals. Canal cruising, an option for the less athletic among us, will be discussed later on.

4

Local Cruising

Goosey goosey Gander,
In my boat I'll wander
Up creeks and down tide
From Essex to the Humber

L IGHT YEARS FROM the racing world are the majority of people who cruise short distances or just potter about in a comparatively narrow geographical area. Not for them the high-tuned, high-tech, highly polished racing boat with its highly polished skipper. It is perhaps the most relaxed form of boating, and includes, at its simplest, casting a little boat off from your own back garden on a pleasant summer day and taking your tea a few miles upwind so that it is not a plug home again.

The ideal short cruise goes like this (assuming you have the ideal short-cruise boat): the weather forecast is anti-cyclonic for the coming week, which does not contain a Bank holiday. Your shopping was done in an almost empty supermarket where all the checkouts were manned and everything you wanted was on special offer, including one of your favourite dishes. Your neighbour is delighted to look after your cat/dog/canary/pot plants while you are away. The awkward relative you felt you must invite is going to a wedding and cannot come, and the charming companion you hardly dared ask is already loading the stores on board along with their own modest requirements in a squashable grip, which when emptied of its contents folds flat under the bunk. Its contents included an offering of your favourite bottle. A couple of hours' gentle sailing take you to a pretty little creek where you drop your anchor and drink your lunch, with a smidgeon of something delicious to soak it up. Basking in the warm sun and lulled by the call of the seabirds, you have a short siesta. A breeze ruffles your hair and awakes you, and you use it for a spanking afternoon's sail to the quay of 'The Jolly Sailor'. You are safe, and hungry, and there is a cabaret, since you are in time to bag the best place in which to watch the newcomers make an enjoyable hash of coming alongside in the rising wind. The pub has good simple food and no juke box, and you fall into your bunk full of good fellowship and fresh air, with the sound of the seabirds to lull you. All these things are part of cruising, but they have rarely happened to us all in one day. One must as always moderate one's expectations. The real world being what it is, the relative will not be asked to a wedding and will turn up with a huge suitcase apparently made of sheet steel with brass bindings, and you'll have to take the dog, as your neighbour is away.

Cruising in home waters

Our definition of local cruising is that you can get home for tea, or spend the weekend away. You can cruise in a sailing boat or in a motor boat, or a combination of the two in a motorsailer, which latter makes a lot of sense for retired persons, for the motor can be a good back-up in case the crew tires.

Motorsailing boats, thank goodness, are not the cumbersome things they once were, for the power/weight ratio of modern engines is such that a really useful unit can be fitted into a sailing boat without completely ruining either her looks or her speed.

There is some splendid cruising to be had round the coast of our British Isles provided one can cope with the reliability of the weather (to be unreliable), can put up with temperatures a little below sunbathing level, and do not mind occasionally getting wet. If it sounds less than appealing, ask yourself why so many spend a lot of time and money doing it. They cannot all be mad. At its most simple level we have had some of our lifetime highlights going off for a day with a picnic in a small boat, mooring up to a clump of reeds for lunch, and sailing back to base in the evening sun. Not very ambitious. Wouldn't make an article for the *Shellback Chronicle*. Many of such pleasures depend on choosing a locality with enough places of interest or charm to last out one's days. In day sailing this would necessitate either an inland water network such as the Broads, or a well protected estuary, such as the Blackwater, Medway or Crouch, or an area protected by islands such as the Minches or the Solent. In other countries there are the Ijsselmeer in Holland, and the Intracoastal Waterway and Long Island Sound in the USA. We have sailed all these areas and they are all enjoyable in their different ways, and the change of scene and people to talk to is refreshing.

There are many other protected sailing grounds on the rivers and lakes of America and Europe that we have not visited.

What type of boat?

This type of pottering can be combined with ownership of a one-design boat of the more traditional type enabling you to have the best of both worlds, some racing and some relaxing sailing. A boat of the half-decker type is probably the best in this respect, and if it is a keel boat then it has the added advantage of a certain stability making it more steady to move around in. There are also a few boats built with a sort of shelter forward and a large cockpit; halfway between the cabin boat and the half-decker. These can be very enjoyable for they are often less tubby than the cabin boat (there is always a tendency for designers to cram too much into a given dimension), and give a better sail. The shelter-boat with its bigger cockpit has the added advantage that it lends itself better to taking friends out for the day; it has more room to sit about without visitors getting in the way of all those ropes, and there is a vestige of shelter in the event of nasty weather. You will rarely see such a boat at a boat show. Few people build them, but they are to be found occasionally, advertised in the local papers, the yachting magazines, and on club notice-boards. Examples among the more racy boats are the Squib, and the Yeoman. Among the non-racing we like the Swift, and the Drascombe Lugger, which with its clones has made some remarkable voyages. This latter applies to the Wayfarer

'A cow to sail ...'

dinghy, but we feel this is on the athletic side. Our list is not meant to be exclusive; it is meant to show how we are thinking.

Linet thought this way when Laurel's parents got too old for *Purple Emperor*. She had the right idea, but they went for the wrong boat, partly due to not sailing in it before they bought it. It had a shelter, it could be trailed behind a small car. It had oars. (They had sailed all their lives without engines, and did not intend to start having one now). It was a hard-chine plywood boat called a Midshipman. It turned out to be a cow to tack, a cow when running or reaching, a cow to row, and a cow to trail. It seemed to be unbalanced in every dimension. Its movement even on inland waters was that of an iron-rimmed bicycle wheel over the Giant's Causeway. Felix gave a rare demonstration of his feelings about it when it burrowed its nose into the reeds for the twentieth time: he got out and walked to the nearest pub, leaving Linet to bring the boat back alone. After that, they did not use it much, and their children disloyally refused to set foot in it. Even Bill, who used occasionally to observe that there were no such things as bad boats, only bad sailors, stopped quoting this adaptation of an old military truism. Moral: do have a trial sail before buying.

Motor boats are enjoyable for local cruising too. When we were young and mad keen on racing, we bought *Petagin* from Sidney Mobbs, who had grown too old to enjoy a good shout. She was a motor boat that we used as a mobile base to tow our boats from regatta to regatta – it wasn't so easy to tow boats by road in those days. She had a long narrow cabin looking just like an old-fashioned tramcar and we occasionally left our little flotilla of racing craft and found ourselves a quiet spot to sunbathe, and boil the kettle on the primus.

However, when most people think of cruising they think of sleeping on board. This can be the least comfortable part of cruising unless you are young and carefree. Bunks are inclined to be narrow, and are sometimes inclined to be inclined. But it is nice not to have to get home by nightfall, to moor to a quiet quay close to a comfortable pub, or in a peaceful anchorage, and have a simple meal followed by a good night's sleep. We will forget for the moment the fishing boat that comes in at 0430 in the pouring rain and wants its berth back, or the rising wind that blows from a direction that makes your chosen spot untenable. Those are among the checks and balances, there is butter-side-down in boats too.

Cruising clubs

One does not have to join a club to go cruising in this way. Probably the majority do not, for how else would you explain the dearth of club burgees around our coasts? But we suggest that in many cases it would pay to do so; that it would increase the value that you would get from the boat, for the more one learns the more one can do. We suspect that a great many of the boats lying untouched week after week in the marinas are owned by those who have not gone deeply enough into the pastime to get full value for time, money and effort. It may be only a lack of confidence, but there is a penetration level that has to be reached to reap the real rewards.

Many of the cruising clubs in Britain are oriented towards the short cruiser, the weekender who might make the occasional holiday voyage across the Channel or the North Sea perhaps, to discover how charming foreigners can be on their home ground. And there are clubs who have cruises-in-company to help those who lack confidence to gain it.

We do not claim to know the existence of all of them. One can get information by reading the Around the Coast feature in *Yachting Monthly*, which has regular reports of activities from the various regions. Perhaps some cruising magazine would consider a Round the Clubs feature on what the cruising clubs are doing.

Clubs that cater for cruising yachtsmen in particular are the Royal Cruising Club, which has a limited and very dedicated membership, the Cruising Association and the Little Ship Club, both the latter being London based with good premises and facilities and in need of members, and further north, the Manchester Cruising Association, which has a very good annual series of lectures, courses and activities centred on Manchester in winter and north Wales in summer. There is also the Royal Naval Sailing Association for anyone with the remotest connection with the Royal Navy; an excellent organisation. We mean the Association, but the description also applies to the latter. Nor must we forget those north of the border: the Clyde Cruising Club is world-renowned, while close to Britain's west the Irish have some good clubs. Some of these are still prefixed by the title Royal, which puzzled us. We asked a member of the Royal St George (!) Yacht Club that we met in Greek waters how the Republic could do this. 'Sure, and it's part of our national history. You cannot deny your history.' How very civilised.

There are other more locally-centred cruising clubs in different places, mostly around the coast, for instance the Lowestoft Cruising Club and the East Anglian Cruising Club. Though in much the same locality, one has a sea-going emphasis, while the other tends to look at the inland waters. Local knowledge is required to root out all these flourishing clubs, and their variations in outlook. If in doubt, find out who is the area representative of the Royal Yachting Association and ask him or her. When the Yacht Racing Association changed its name and acronym it claimed it would help the cruising yachtsman too. It does try, and only if the cruising folk keep on at it will it improve.

Almost all the local clubs with a cruising background that we have encountered have a positive educational function as well as a social. Quite apart from the traditional method of learning (watch what Fred does, then try it yourself), many have excellent programmes of lectures and courses in aspects of the crafts of sailing and navigation, together with meteorology.

Cruising clubs as such are not so numerous in other countries, except that the USA has two of the best. The Cruising Club of America is roughly parallel with Britain's Royal Cruising Club. It got diverted into ocean racing in the days when ocean racers were basically cruisers who liked the occasional race (it organised the Bermuda Race, for example). That sport has now evolved too far, and the CCA is once again mainly a real cruising club. There is also the Seven Seas Cruising Association, open to persons of all nationalities who live aboard and cruise their boat; a very friendly outfit.

Formal qualifications
The British, sailors to the backbone, cherish a freedom that allows anyone at all, competent or not, to go to sea in charge of a pleasure boat without any permit or licence of any kind.

This right is under challenge from our over-regulated allies in the EEC. They have some cause. At one time the seagoing community could tolerate the few incompetents and lunatics that they came across, but the great expansion of yachting in all its forms has increased the probability of encountering them to a worrying level. The government, not wishing to offend the traditionalist lobby, introduced a form of qualification administered and examined by the Royal Yachting Association. After some hiccups this is now running very well. It awards 'tickets' at various levels of examined ability, and is therefore already in being in case the EEC becomes more demanding. With deaths caused by careless pleasure-boat drivers increasing throughout Europe, (and some are the fault of the British, it must be said), the possibility of compulsory certificates becomes very likely.

Most cruising clubs run courses to help their members qualify. Some are better than others, but the best are very good indeed, and would alone make these clubs worth the subscription. We strongly advise anyone planning a lot of sailing to obtain the yachtmaster qualification. The 'Offshore' is usually enough. It does *not* make you into some form of instant shellback: but it is evidence that you are responsible, that you care, and that you have a basic knowledge and ability, and will go on to acquire the experience that will make you a real seaman or woman. The best way of qualifying in practice is to go on an instructional cruise to be followed by the RYA examination. While this is not cheap, it costs no more than most holidays, and look at the bonus you get. Usually the instruction is good, and friends have told us it makes a most rewarding and challenging vacation.

Qualifications in most other countries are very formalised. In the USA, which still retains some basic freedoms, qualifications are not yet mandatory, as far as we know. The US Coast Guard help you to acquire them. They are very helpful to amateurs, both in a practical way as nursemaids to those in difficulties, and also to those wishing to further their skills and thus avoid getting into difficulties.

Where to cruise

One of the best areas for short-haul cruising, and one where we cut our yachting teeth, is the Norfolk Broads. These have been a centre of nautical fun and games for a very long time; the Royal Norfolk and Suffolk Yacht Club is one of the oldest in Britain, dating back to 1851, but the local Water Frolics have their origins centuries ago.

There are two ways to enjoy pottering about the Broads. One can have a cottage in the vicinity, perhaps a waterside one if you can afford it (they fetch a good price), and have a dayboat to make short forays into darkest Norfolk, taking one's lunch or tea. Or you can have a cruising boat of an appropriate sort.

The Broads have developed their own style of motor cruiser that is well suited to these waters, though it would be unwise to take them to sea. Of lowish freeboard, so that the sides do not tower over the low banks and make boarding difficult (and also a lot less dangerous if anyone is unfortunate enough to fall in), they are extremely comfortable inside, with most of the facilities one would expect in a simple cottage. They are not difficult to drive, being very manoeuvrable, but they would be even better if they had a conning position aft instead of forward; it is always better to steer from aft, you get a better idea of any tendency of the boat to swing about.

The traditional Broads sailing cruiser is a lovely boat. Our families have owned two, and we remember some of our happiest times in them. They are over-canvassed by sea-going standards, but in the calm waters that is not a great danger; one can always reduce sail. They have the ability to go about on the proverbial sixpence; these boats were a long way ahead of the current sea-going fashion in having separately hung, balanced rudders right aft, and they can tack up narrow rivers that are barely as wide as twice the boat's length. There is an easily-acquired technique for it. Their masts are stepped in tabernacles and have a counterweight on the foot so that they can be lowered with ease. It was our pride to approach a low bridge under sail, to furl sail, lower the mast, shoot the bridge, raise the mast and sails and to continue sailing without the boat coming to a stop, or needing any help from oars or quant pole. Neither of our boats had an engine, nor did we really need one, though nowadays most of the craft do have an auxiliary.

In those days boats were wooden, and most were old (our *Barracuda* had been built in 1896). They tended to have low head-room, mainly because their hulls were not deep in the water, but this was alleviated when moored by an ingenious raising cabin top that was simple to put up and down.

Nowadays, there are modern reproductions of these old boats made with glassfibre hulls, but finished in traditional styles.

All boats on the Broads must conform to strict pollution regula-tions. These did not exist in our day, and the waters did not seem that dirty; there were plenty of fish, in fact one of the hazards of sailing in those days lay in avoiding the millions of anglers who were presum-ably there because of the multitude of fish. Now the boats must have holding tanks for their sewage and are required to discharge at approved pump-out stations, but there are plenty of these and this does not seem to us an unreasonable obligation. We understand that boats not equipped with auxiliary engines are exempt from the hold-ing tank rule; if so this is an eminently sensible concession: there are very few pure sailing boats these days, and one can imagine circum-stances that would present a becalmed crew with a fearful choice of horrors.

Some people say that the Norfolk Broads are overcrowded. While *Hosanna* was being slipped at Great Yarmouth we hired a sailing boat and had a wet and windy old time sailing our childhood haunts; a really hairy beat up to the Pleasure Boat Inn at Hickling is in our memory. We did not see any evidence that the Broads are overcrowded (except by swans) compared with the 1960s. We saw few boats, though it was summer, and were inconvenienced by no-one. With the rise in popularity of the package foreign holiday it seems that the Broads hire fleets have been reduced, as environmentalists (and swans) increased.

One of the pleasant features of Broads sailing is the series of open regattas or Water Frolics as they are called. These go back centuries and pre-date organised yacht-racing as we know it now. At a typical one there are not only races for yachts, including the lovely old cruis-ers, but there are rowing races, greasy poles, pillow-fights on rafts, and with any luck some madman to wheelbarrow across a tight-rope suspended over the water. The whole village is en boisterous fête.

Some of the owners of the Broads cruisers take their racing quite seriously, and there are regular week-end races for these boats under the flag of the Norfolk Broads Yacht Club at Wroxham. The sight of a couple of dozen of these large craft crowding the line on a windy day is daunting but thank the Lord they are very manoeuvrable and accidents are rare. We recall one incident when one of the larger boats racing in the narrow river Bure was taken by a sudden urge to gybe while abreast of several other boats. Pushed to the riverside as she was, her swinging boom neatly took the legs from under a gentleman who was mowing the lawn in front of his riverside cottage, and carted him off. There are hazards to riverside gardening in Norfolk. Cows, too, can be surprised by a thwack on the rump by a gybing boom. This is sailing at close quarters, and the misses are nicely judged. The hairsbreadth between boats racing on the Broads would cause cardiac arrest in many an ocean sailor used to plenty of sea room. Some sea sailors sneer at Broadsmen; but as someone experienced at sea as well as the Broads, Bill has a very deep respect for the standards of boat handling typical among the good Broadsmen. If some sea-going yachtsmen would or could match it they would be better seamen.

We used to take our dog sailing with us on the Broads. He was called Pilot, which is the traditional nickname for the navigator in the Navy, and Bill had spent much of his life being summoned by a cry of 'Pilot!' He decided to get his own back on the dog. Pilot would occasionally be taken short while we were beating to windward up a river, and as we swung the stern in to the bank while tacking he would leap ashore to relieve himself, run on to about the right place and leap back aboard when we next tacked close to that bank.

When we raced, the skipper of one of our rivals, the big black cutter *Forester*, once brought a large bone, and when our two yachts were in close quarters tried to entice the dog Pilot to leap across to their boat. This would have entailed our disqualification, as a racing yacht is obliged to finish with all its crew still on board. Needless to say, the faithful Keeshond turned his nose up at these shenanigans, which exemplified the spirit of fun in which the racing was conducted. It was not like the Royal Ocean Racing Club, where they take life seriously.

There are two very sociable cruising clubs for these sailing craft, the East Anglian Cruising Club, and the Yare Valley Sailing Club. There are also a good number of other clubs on the Broads organising racing of one sort or another as well as social activities.

There are many other watery acres where boats congregate and happy, safe, and easy sailing is available, on lakes or reservoirs, or sheltered estuaries and rivers.

Abroad

In Holland there is the Ijsselmeer, which we British still think of as the Zuider Zee. It is cruised by thousands of well handled, very well kept yachts. The Ijsselmeer is more of an inland sea, and its very size, 560 square miles, gives it some of the sea's characteristics. It is very shallow, about four to five metres at most, and this shallowness combined with the open area can produce some uncomfortable short waves in strong winds, and some very exciting sailing. It is possible to sail or cruise in the more sheltered parts in bad weather, but it must be said that even though it is not tidal, it is not so foolproof a cruising ground as the Broads.

The Dutch are very hospitable, they build good boats, they know how to look after boats, and Holland is very close to the UK by both air and ferry. Many British are nowadays keeping their boats in France because proprietors of marinas in England have unreasonably exploited a shortage of marina berths and raised mooring fees to unjustifiable levels. Boat owners could as well keep their boats in Holland, where conditions in our view are better. We have never been enamoured of the mooring provisions in many French marinas (the mother chain and piglet system which we think inconvenient and fundamentally flawed, especially so for the shorthanded and elderly), and they are becoming more expensive all the time.

There are other areas of the world where some good cruising can be had in sheltered waters, and where the living conditions are attractive. That part of the Greek Ionian Sea, called the Inland Sea by the local British, is one example; it is the area south of the island of Levkas, sheltered from the open sea by Kephalonia, Ithaca, and Zakinthos, to which must be added the Gulf of Corinth. This is one of the most attractive parts of Greece, and the sea is seldom rough enough to

The authors' barge Hosanna *at Meganisi.*

worry the crockery. Note the word seldom: we have one or two rough rides in our memories.

In the USA there are parts of the Intracoastal Waterway, the regions round Pamlico Sound, for example, where the sailing is good and well-protected. The Chesapeake Bay is so too, but is also big enough to frighten the life out of you, and should be treated with more caution: any body of water approaching 200 miles in length has the capacity to conjure up some respectable waves.

Other areas such as the Abacos in the Bahamas, or the Barrier Reef in Queensland, Australia, have their disadvantages in the form of the occasional very, very bad storm. These areas are not for the inexperienced, and neither is the Baltic.

Long Island Sound and its adjacent waters would be a good cruising ground if a million others had not got there first. Just try getting in a word edgeways on Channel 16 (the distress or calling channel) on a fine Sunday off the coast of New England and you will see what we mean.

There are other less obvious areas that one can enjoy. Many people like the Balearics, though they are not to our taste, (see remarks above about Long Island Sound). This area too is not without its weather problems. It is not as sheltered as some of the others we have mentioned, and can feel the effects of the *mistral* blowing in the Gulf of Lions.

Boats for local cruising

Let us now consider some of the more desirable features of boats for elder persons to go short-term cruising.

Choose a boat with good initial stability, that is with a fairly good beam for the weight. In our view initial stability is more important to persons past their physical prime than the ultimate righting moments of a boat knocked over to ninety degrees. We are talking here of sailing in semi-sheltered waters, or perhaps the occasional open passage in a period of settled fine weather. Retired people do not have to be back at work on Monday, and they can and should wait until it is prudent before venturing into potentially rough water.

Open boats should have good seating, and the ability to set and furl sail without getting out on to a rather vulnerable little foredeck. Larger boats with cabins should also have a good cockpit in which the crew can sit at ease. There should be an easy entry into the cabin; shoe horns should not be necessary to get oneself below. There should be hand-holds and railings wherever they are needed.

You need to consider an easily set rig; some form of roller furling and/or reefing is desirable, and if the sails can be managed entirely from the security of the cockpit, then that is a very good point.

Watch the locker spaces. The elderly are not so good at getting on their knees to reach the backs of inaccessible lockers, or heaving up heavy cushions and wooden lids to get things from under seats. Well-running drawers are much to be preferred, preferably installed so that they pull out fore and aft, when they probably will not need retainers.

It should be possible to pick up moorings from the cockpit. If your chosen cruising ground will necessitate a lot of anchoring, then no matter how small the cruising boat, consider a self-stowing anchor with an electric windlass; some very neat little ones are made nowadays, and we should not be heaving around 30-odd pounds of heavy metal at our age. Even if you wish to use a fibre anchor cable, do not forget that anchors can require a strong pull to break them out.

For this type of cruising we feel that a marina berth is no bad thing. The ability to board and disembark simply and safely is important. And so is the reassurance that your boat is safe during gales, and that you do not have to dress up in your oilskins in the middle of the night and grovel about in mud to 'see if she is all right' on her buoy mooring. (Or perhaps you are a natural worrier and that is the aspect of boat husbandry that appeals to you! If so, go to it!) But there is one aspect of marinas that can be awkward for the elderly, and that is that car parking is often a long distance from the berths. Not only that, but sometimes there are finger pontoons that are long, unsteady, encumbered with projecting cleats and fittings, difficult to walk on, and impossible to push a trolley along. And some sort of trolley access is desirable, for boats often need heavy items manhandled on board. Marina designers: please think a little more of these things.

We do not think it is necessary to be over-particular about the internal accommodation of boats in this category. One is not aboard for extended periods, and minor discomforts can yield to other considerations, perfection being unattainable. But try for as much comfort as you can, it helps when you are tired or the weather turns bad, and be sure that the galley is safe and easy to use.

Generally, boats in this category will be production boats, often reviewed in the yachting press. Unfortunately, the magazines seem to send out trial teams of bright young men to test the boats. How seldom is even a token experienced woman taken to see if the galley really works, (we bet the trial team only makes tea) or if the bunks can be made up without skinning your knuckles. We have never, ever seen in any magazine, any reference to the suitability or otherwise of any boat for ancient mariners of either sex. Editors: please rectify; we are a considerable market.

5

~~~~~~~~~~

Working with Boats

Half a pound of twopenny nails
Half a pint of teak oil
A mooring warp and some courtesy flags
And the latest Heikell

W E KNOW SEVERAL examples of persons retiring who have started
some commercial enterprise associated with yachting. Some have
bought chandlers' shops, for instance. These are quite often offered for
sale in the yachting magazines. As the viability of these enterprises
depends on the location as well as the possible clientele, no firm opinion can be expressed on whether or not such a business is viable. It is
after all a form of specialist retailing, and we would think that anyone
without experience of this type of business would need to think twice.
Do you want to tie up your time in this way? The winter is quiet, but
from fitting-out time (usually March) and all summer you will be busy,
just when you might like to do something else with the good weather.

Another business that many people dream of having in their retirement is a boatyard. Bill's family were mixed up in this many years ago,
in those leisurely days when a small yard could give a modest living for
a man and a boy because all boats were built to order; each builder had
his own type of boat, and very seldom built anything novel. Methods
were tried, tested and costed, we had a stable economy and above all,
there was very little government interference with industry.

It is very different nowadays. Boatbuilders and boat-repairers lead a
troubled life. The price of material varies almost from day to day, interest rates change at ministerial whim, old-established suppliers go into
liquidation, and worst of all, so do customers, leaving their bills
unpaid. One of our friends says that his solicitor's bills are one of his
major overhead costs.

One of Bill's old school friends, who had a career as director of a
major manufacturing company, bought a 25% share in a famous yard.

Degrees in Business Administration made no difference; it went under. Bill is eternally grateful that when he left the Royal Navy, Laurel vetoed his suggestion that his gratuity should be used to start a boatyard. Boats are for pleasure, she said, not business.

We bought a boat.

Other friends have converted an old cargo barge into a barge-hotel, and operate on the French canals. There are four double cabins for guests, and they maintain a high standard of comfort on board with a shady deck-terrace, and a good dining room. They have a minibus which liaises with the boat so that at various stops they can take their customers to see local sights.

There are a lot of these hotel barges operating, ranging from the deluxe to the squalid, and many of them go bust in no time at all because their operators are dreamers and have no business sense. Our friends have sold out now after several successful and happy years, but it has to be said that they worked very hard and did not make a fortune; even the successful ones do not keep much ahead of the break-even point; one should have alternative incomes to fall back on.

Running a business overseas offers, in theory, the best of both worlds. Good weather, and what may seem at first sight a less prodnosing type of government. Unless you know your chosen country well, however, there are pitfalls galore.

A major problem for expatriates trying to run a business in a foreign country is a lack of understanding of business methods and etiquette in the country concerned. Whatever one may believe about the common market and so-called level playing fields, each EEC country has very different commercial practices, and all have a somewhat chauvinistic attitude to foreign competition on their doorstep. All right if you are working hard and not succeeding, but any signs of success has the local mafia looking to their underhand methods. No! we are not being paranoid. There are exceptions galore, but there are very many examples of what we have just described, especially in the Mediterranean countries, and one or two in the Caribbean. Are you fully into the delicacies of 'buying' your permits to trade? Do you know the 'phakilaki' etiquette, and how to enclose one with your application? (*Phakilaki* is the Greek for a little envelope; its significance should be obvious).

In general terms we would advise against starting a business from scratch on retirement. If you have good experience of the trade it is a different matter, but in that case you are not strictly retiring. Something that can be run part-time would prevent you from atrophying, and give you time to enjoy some leisure, which you have well deserved. On the other hand, helping out with someone else's business could provide occupation and interest, but that is a different game of water-polo.

Noah was 500 years old when he begat Shem, Ham, and Japhet. He was 600 when he built the Ark. So his sons were centenarian shipwrights.

PART TWO

In Up to Your Middle

6

Half-the-time Cruising

One, two, find your crew,
Three, four, provision and store,
Five, six, learn how it ticks,
Seven, eight, cruising's great,
Nine, ten, back safe again.

PEOPLE WHO RETIRE to devote themselves to cruising usually fall into two distinct camps. Some take the plunge hook, line and sinker, and enthusiastically go to sea. Their boat is their home, and they live in it winter and summer, probably finding a safe harbour for the winter months. They feel healthy and confident, perhaps they have had plenty of experience and see no reason why advancing years should affect their ability to make voyages.

Many more people favour an approach which envisages some time at sea and some on shore. Often the other half of the decision-making team exerts pressure for a compromise, and why not?

You could have many reasons for choosing this solution. It may be the right one if your health is less than perfect: sailing need not stop if you have the facilities to check up at sensible intervals. Your life may be enriched with other activities besides sailing, and you may feel that winter is the time for these pursuits. You have a point.

Frankly, living aboard a small boat in winter, even in the Med, is not entirely a bed of roses. (It has its compensations, especially when bad weather causes power breakdowns ashore, and you on board are happily generating your own power, and are the only people with light, heat, and cooking.) Winter is not comfortable unless the boat is very carefully arranged and the mooring is very carefully selected. The

41

option to cruise continuously all the year round might sound attractive, but there is no doubt that it is wearing, and a winter rest from
cruising may be not only beneficial, but looked forward to. What we
are going into here are alternatives that a compromise might lead to.

Boat and cottage mode

Cruising in the summer months and spending the winter doing something else supposes that there will be living accommodation for the
winter, and that the boat will be laid up. We meet many people working out their nautical ambitions by these means, and it can make very
good sense for the retired.

The usual way (if you do not keep your original home) is to have a
villa, flat or cottage somewhere that becomes your home in winter. To
get the most out of this particular situation means thorough research
beforehand. This type of sailing does not take up more than a part of
one's time and therefore the locality should be chosen for reasons
other than navigation. It would be unsettling to find oneself with some
wonderful sailing, but to be bored stiff when not in the boat, to find
one's neighbours were not to one's taste, and that in winter the whole
place shut down and went skiing in Val d'Isère. The cottage is fixed,
the boat is mobile, so the site of the former is more important. Choose
your country, and get to know it and its language first. Explore a good
deal. Find out about things. Good choices result from a wide selection,
and a knowledge of what to choose. It is necessary to define your aim
and then narrow it down to the essentials. This process is nine-tenths
of choosing.

Let us examine the advantages of this option:

- The cottage can be let in summer to enhance one's income.
- It becomes a base where you can leave bulky possessions.
- The medical and dental facilities will be well-known to you (you
  will have checked up on them if you are not already familiar) and
  where psychological and practical support from neighbours and
  friends is available if you need it.
- You can follow some quite different hobby which one or both of
  you might like quite as much as sailing.

Note that if you let the property in summer you will need to find
somewhere to lock up your valuables. A stout garage with a heavy
steel door might suffice, as in summer the garage is less likely to be
needed by your tenants.

If you do not let your cottage, the above still applies. Absent owners
bring eager thieves.

The advantages of having a winter base on land are very real ones.
One of the problems of long-term continuous cruising arises when a

personal disaster of an unresolved nature strikes. It may never do so, and if it does, is not necessarily of one's own making or being: one's children can be in difficulty and require your presence, but more often such problems will involve yourselves, and can include temporary illnesses, injury, or a need for dental care. At these times it is consoling to have a depot. However well the rest of the grotty-yotties rally round in an emergency when you are sailing, and they do so very well as a rule, it is disconcerting to be vulnerable in an isolated community where the facilities are rural, and where there are language problems and little or no communications. It has to be taken into account that when an older person falls ill, he or she becomes a rallying point for all the well-intentioned busybodies in creation. Bill believes that every time a stranger over sixty gets a splinter in his finger the local hospital prepares the intensive care unit and Age Concern puts out a red alert. When you are on familiar ground it is easier to exert one's own point of view, and those familiar with you are more familiar with your eccentricities. They know you always have splinters in your finger on Wednesdays at fitting-out time.

There is no need for the cottage to be at the sea-side (unless you wish to look after your boat in the same spot, in which case see the villa/marina option below as well). There are many arguments why it should not be. The first of these is financial, for being the proverbial stone's throw from the sea will more than double the price of the property. On the other hand a seaside cottage is easy to let.

Abroad or at home?
By having a cottage in the UK you retain a better title to the National Health Service, which may be less marvellous than it once was, but still has its points. You would be in a country where you know the language and can cope with builders, gas men, telephone engineers, and above all, the bureaucracy, for having a property anywhere in the world is to engage the attention of the *petit fonctionnaire*, a more all-embracing title than civil servant which the French have devised for the miscellaneous prodnoses, nigglers and welfare workers who want to improve your life for you whether you want it improved (their definition) or not. That is the down side of the equation, because even coping with these people brings stress. Ve haf vays of making you 'appy, no? Well, no.

Still fancy a cottage? Abroad, perhaps?

Obviously in England, even with the fall in house prices which made such headlines throughout 1992, you would pay serious money for a cottage in the south, which has by far the highest residential prices in Europe, if not in the world. We could buy a nice waterside property in New England for half the price of one in Old England.

Prices of property in the better parts of France are not very different to those obtaining in south-east England, but there are many other less fashionable places.

Old or new buildings? You can get old barns and cottages in rural France for very little, but there would be a lot of work to be done, which would take time. You might enjoy this. But beware! Ask yourself why the village or hamlet in question has been abandoned. Often these properties which look so lovely in the sunshine are appalling in winter, which is when you will be there.

The villa/marina option

This is an alternative that might suit you. Instant apartments with waterfront to moor your boat are now widely available and glowingly advertised in Spain, France and Italy; indeed most Mediterranean marinas are built with the boat/villa combination in mind, to the point where building villas and apartments usually takes precedence over provision of good facilities for the boats, there being more profit in property, and cheapjack architects more common than good marina designers. There is something very beguiling about the idea of your boat nodding at its blue Mediterranean mooring a step away from your shaded terrace. At its best this is a wonderful solution, but be sure to visit the place in both winter and summer before you decide. This will reassure you that the windows fit well enough to keep out sand and wind from the winter gales sweeping in from the no longer blue sea, that despite the tiled floors you can keep warm in cold weather, and that all the shops do not close out of season. You will also ascertain that in summer the place and the neighbours are congenial to those who might rent it in your absence. Check the boat moorings as well as the villa; cheapjacks can save money on the parts that are under water, relying on the fact that more people can assess a property than can assess underwater fittings.

Be on guard: these commercial developments are designed down to a price. The architects expect that in the main they will be occupied only in the summer months so they may be built with inferior materials. Most of them are poorly insulated, have no heating, and can be uncomfortably cold and damp in winter. Further, the architects are likely to be partially correct: most of the flats will be empty all winter and the ambience will be that of a dead and windy city from which the inhabitants have fled as if fearing the plague. Nine out of ten shops will be closed, and the tenth will have little to offer except hope of a new season in a few months' time. The car parks, in winter, will consist of acres of empty tarmac across which the odd pieces of litter gambol like tumbleweed in Texas, and the only visitors will be the gangs of professional thieves who ritually tour these developments each winter seeking what they may devour. Do your research carefully and be observant. Ask lots of questions. Ask in the supermarkets *when* they close for the winter. (To ask *if* invites an equivocal reply, whereas the right question usually elicits a date, and then you know where you are.) They will all tell you that they reopen for Easter, and this is as vague as it is inaccurate.

It occurs to us that we are sounding rather downbeat about a perfectly good mode of life. In this chapter we are going to assume the virtues and pleasures of the life to be self-evident. What the person who has not travelled so much, or who has not had the time to observe places out of season needs, we feel, is to be made aware of the snags. There are always snags in everything: they are there to be overcome.

Weather in winter, and other worries

The cottage need not, of course, be in Europe or the Med. You could be warmer in winter in a house in south-west England or the southern United States, than in the Med, though in Britain you will get less sunshine. Once you leave the seaside in the Med and go inland the winter temperature falls noticeably because the Med is a landlocked sea, and only its shores are influenced by the retained warmth of the water. Most of the bordering countries are mountainous. As we sat writing this, anchored in a bay on the island of Levkas on the west coast of Greece, we were under a beetling snow-capped hill rather higher than the tallest mountain in England, and opposite on the mainland we could clearly see the snow which was lying well down the hillsides. The wind blew down the television transmitter on the mainland opposite a couple of nights later.

Looking at the weather map of Europe that the television shows (when the transmitter has not been blown down and when the boat is pointing in the right direction), the temperature in England in winter quite often exceeds that of the east coast of Greece, and mostly exceeds that in the interior. It rains in the Ionian winter. How it rains! We had recently more rain in a day than East Anglia would get in a month. On the other hand, the winter is short (we ate lunch out of doors until mid-November), and includes many bright sunny days, and it does not get dark at four o'clock as it can do in northern climes.

If you take your boat to the Intracoastal Waterway you must leave the New England states in October and go south, or you will be stuck in the ice. Not till you get well into Florida or the Bahamas will you find any warmth in winter. We once crossed from Georgia into Florida in January. We were all wrapped up in jerseys and oilskins before a bitingly cold north wind, and were amused to find a 'Welcome Station' manned (if that is the right word) by a pretty young lady in a low-cut sun suit dispensing complimentary iced orange juice. Poor dear, low cut dresses do not go with goose pimples, and the electric heater hidden behind her stand had pinkened her calves but the rest of her was blue with cold. At Easter, however, Florida became pleasantly warm.

The parts of the Med that are noticeably warmer in winter are quite numerous and mostly depend on local climatic anomalies. Thus Gibraltar can be miserable in winter (we lived there once), while the Spanish coast to the eastward generally enjoys a much better climate. In the Balearics, Ibiza, and to a lesser extent Mallorca, are warmer in winter than Minorca, which seems to get the tail end of the Gulf of Lions' *mistrals* and *tramontanes*, as do the more northern parts of the Spanish east coast.

Along the coast of France, the littoral from the Spanish border is cold in winter, except for a short band in the lee of the Pyrénées Orientales. This low-lying Languedoc coast is ravaged by *tramontane* and *mistral* winds at frequent intervals, though the latter wind is strongest in the Camargue at the mouth of the Rhône, where it is reputed to blow the horns off the bulls. It is a wind that has to be experienced in its full screaming horror down the valley of the Rhône to be understood. The *mistral* is felt along the coast to about Le Lavandou, where it is beginning to lose heart. Further east the coast is protected by the Alpes Maritimes, a high mountain range which slopes down to a coast which becomes something of a sun trap.

This benign coast extends over the border into Italy, though we have found the Italian Riviera slightly less congenial than the French from all points of view. Both areas are expensive, the coastal land being limited. A house there will be much the same price as a similar size one in parts of London. A further complication is that so many foreigners are moving in that some of the more attractive villages are firmly resisting further incursions. There are already 30 000 English speakers in the French Riviera.

Corsica and Sardinia have less benign, but not intolerable, winter climates on their coasts. Corsica is apt to be a bit wind-ravaged, especially on its west coast, and has a big disadvantage in that the loonier natives have a hobby of blowing up property belonging to foreigners, believing that it will endear them to everybody and further their quest for independence. Nothing in Corsica is as cheap as on the mainland, but that goes for most islands. Sardinia has no virulent independence movement. It is poor and backward, but EEC money is flooding in and holiday properties are going up everywhere. The southern end is the more benign, but all its coasts are inclined to be windy in winter.

Sicily does not have the warm climate that you would suppose, though the south coast is warmer if more socially backward. One of the features of having property in any part of Italy is the necessity of coping with the state religion, which is theft. We have visited many private houses in Italy where the security arrangements are akin to those of the Tower of London, and evidently better than Buckingham Palace. In Sicily the thieves manifest not only as organized crime, but also in active amateur and juvenile leagues; little urchins barely big enough to toddle will nick anything that is not welded down. If it is welded they will tell their dads, who will come back with cutting gear.

Malta, off Sicily's south coast, is a reasonable winter spot and well used to coping with English-speaking visitors. The climate is not bad, the only blot being the dreaded *gregale*, a north-east wind which blows across the Ionian Sea bringing an icy blast all the way from the mountains of Yugoslavia. A disadvantage of Malta is that it is small, and one's movements are a little restricted, but it has good air services, and a tolerable car ferry to Sicily. Lovers of natural beauty will have a hard time; the land itself is stony and barren and there are very few trees, though the flowers in spring are lovely. (We once lived there, too.)

Italy itself has its points. The west coast is a little warmer in winter than the east, but cooler than the Riviera. The cool band extends well south of Rome, but the coast south of Naples can be quite tolerable. We spent a winter in the western part of the Gulf of Taranto (accent the first syllable) and it was not at all bad, though Taranto itself was noticeably cooler and windier (and indescribably scruffy), as was the whole of Puglia (the Heel). The east coast of Italy has a continental climate rather like Yugoslavia, and this is even more marked up near Venice at the head of the Adriatic, where the winters can be almost Arctic. Italy is, despite this, beautiful, historic, and blessed with a musical language and works of art and buildings beyond price. Food in the markets is no dearer than in France, but for some reason is much more expensive once it gets to the restaurants.

Greece should not be considered as having a good winter climate. The Aegean has many very severe gales, and the Ionian has a lot of rain, and both have quite low temperatures at night unless there is a south wind. Much the same applies to Aegean Turkey. Istanbul and the Black Sea are very cold in winter, and though it warms up as one moves south, one has to be well south of Izmir to feel comfortable. We spent a winter in Bodrum and had a lovely time, but the boat was covered in snow for a day or two. (The same applies to Rome, Athens, Antibes, Aigues-Mortes, and Ampuria Brava; in all these places we have had snow on the deck, usually just for a few hours. The local people all said it was exceptional. But how exceptional if it has happened at so many places, though admittedly over fifteen years.) Round Cape Krio, the south-west tip of Turkey, the weather improves. (Krio,

The port of Mirina on the island of Limnos. Our sailing barge
Hosanna *is in centre stage. This was late July – who says the Greek
islands are overcrowded?*

please note, is the Greek for cold.) Cyprus, apparently has a benign
winter climate. That is possibly because we have never wintered
there.

It would be nice to report on the Lebanon and Israel, but they must
be a bit out of the reckoning for the time being. Israel has a pleasant
climate close to the coast. Egypt has a very good winter climate, but
they do not seem to extend a welcome to other than short-term visitors on organised tours. The bureaucracy is mind-boggling, and the
menace of the ever-outstretched hand demanding baksheesh at every
turn is very off-putting. Europeans not able to afford the luxury dis-
tricts there could suffer from acute culture shock.

Tunisia has a good winter climate. This is the more politically stable
part of North Africa, and where we have felt less ill-at-ease. By and
large to invest substantially in property anywhere along the African
coast would require unusual optimism as well as great care and a
sound knowledge of the place and people.

Indeed, a locality for a winter cottage anywhere abroad needs
selecting with care. You will need, we suggest, some contact with other
expatriates. You may scoff at this for the moment, thinking perhaps
that you are already fed up with your own compatriots and can think
of nothing better than to get away from them, but in practical matters

the expatriate community can help each other quite a bit. We assume you have not been brought up in the foreign country to the extent that you know it intimately. To live there is going to involve close and frequent contact with its bureaucracy, occasionally a detailed understanding and knowledge of its etiquette, traditions and methods, and a group of people can pool their experiences to mutual benefit.

There are many books written to guide the British or the American through the minefield of European administrations, but they can seldom foresee all that you will come up against. Not that the authorities in these countries are habitually oppressive, beastly to foreigners, or even less than helpful, but it is difficult to understand all the nuances. Words often have shades of meaning or legal interpretations that do not appear even in the best inter-language dictionaries, and most countries (though not, for reasons that are beyond us, Britain) take the reasonable view that a person coming to live in their land should learn their language.

Problems get worse when considering other more exotic destinations. Those countries which once enjoyed the blessings of being a British colony are nowadays beginning to forget their lessons in administration. Others have never enjoyed these benefits and do not want to hear about them. Of course the ex-British colonies do tend to have a knowledge of the English tongue.

Anywhere east of Sicily has to be thought of as the Levant in business matters. Naif and innocent Europeans used to ethical practices must be wary if wishing to buy property. The goalposts are not just movable, they are in a different football field from the start.

Property is a field for the professional. So make a short list of the places in which you have an interest, and then find the experts, High Street agents, advertisers in the quality Sunday papers; some of them must be straight and knowledgeable.

We would counsel making a motor tour of your shortlisted areas before showing more than a preliminary interest. Make the tour at Easter or in early November; this way there is some chance of getting an idea of both the summer and winter conditions, for often at these times the places are in transition. A reputable agent with local, on-the-spot representation clearly has advantages.

We would want a lot of convincing that time-share or condominium property is worth considering.

Renting locally
There is a variation on the cottage solution to cruising half-yearly. It is not much used by the British, though we have found that the French and the Americans are taking to it. This is to lay up the boat for the winter in some congenial spot and to move into a locally-rented flat or

small hotel, and to use this as a base for exploratory excursions into the winter hinterland.

This is a solution not likely to lend itself to the impecunious living on very little. Generally it is adopted by those with a good pension, such as airline pilots or admirals and such persons do exist, and they go sailing in their retirement. We are writing for all types. It is also a possible solution for a temporary period, a couple of years, say. Several people we know go land cruising in the winter, in what the States call a motorhome, and we call a motor-caravan. One could at a pinch live in a properly fitted caravan for the winter, but then, why not the boat?

This policy enables one to have the best of both worlds, for one can change cruising ground each year and be almost as mobile as the year-round yottie. The boat can be smaller, but this means that some baggage has to be left in store to be sent on to next winter's base, a serious disadvantage. A large enough caravan could act as a store in summer, but it could be better to have a larger boat and have some of it equipped as a hold to carry with you your winter extras. The hire market for consumer durables that the British and Americans are used to is not very well developed in some parts of Europe, and is non-existent in some of the nicer tourist areas.

You may ask: why not make a quick trip back to last year's winter base to get the baggage, pick up the car, and drive to the new one? Why not? Well, one reason is the comparative difficulty of getting about the Med from one holiday area directly to another. Nearly all airline services operate between the holiday areas and major centres of population, and they almost all pack up from October to March. And then, do you want to own a car or caravan? A car is a documented encumbrance that is under the eye of authorities everywhere. In one country you may keep it for six months, in another three only. Cars are a major focus for petty crime everywhere. It is sometimes difficult to arrange secure garaging and custody in the summer while you are away cruising. And its price represents a large asset tied up at risk and not used for half, at least, of its life.

There are other solutions to the car problem. The first is to buy an old banger each winter, take out the minimum third party insurance, and to leave it behind when you move on. The total purchase price is likely to be less than the depreciation on the day you drive a new car from the showroom. It is not very likely to be stolen, especially if you paint it a conspicuous yellow (which also enables you to find it in hypermarket car parks), and from our experience is quite likely to be as reliable as a new one. If it is not, then write it off and get another; you will still be better off financially. You must, however, be prepared to view your car merely as a convenient tool of living; you have to disqualify it as a status symbol, or alternatively use it to demonstrate that you are above status symbols.

The second solution is to hire or lease a car either for the whole winter or on an as-required basis. In holiday resorts the price of car hire can often be negotiated very advantageously in the winter months, especially if you are likely to be a good customer over a period. Unfortunately some countries have special number plates on hire cars, which makes them conspicuous to thieves.

Because any apartment to be rented for shortish periods is likely to be in a holiday area, it will consequently have a reasonable rent, especially for a tenant who can be relied upon to quit in spring. But the usual disadvantages of holiday homes for winter living apply with equal force. The heating will be inadequate and the insulation likewise, though these defects are not apparent when you first move in. A couple adopting this policy in Levkas last winter found their roof leaked and the rooms were flooded. The flat had tile floors and it does not rain in summer - why repair the roof?

It is better to rent a normal house, though even here they are likely to be fitted for summer occupation. Of course the landlord will promise to provide this or that during the winter. He will not. He is not a criminal, he just does not rate the obligation very highly. You were obviously tired or excited when you made the request and he said yes to calm you down, not with any intention of actually providing the items. Everybody knows you do not have extra heating in a holiday home. And of course the Med is not cold like Scotland, Sweden, Canada, etc, he consoles himself while going home to his roaring olivewood fire.

One can move into a modest hotel, though we are told that often the better bargains can be had from the more up-market hotels that remain open to a small handful of customers and who believe that some occupancy encourages other business. In any event you might want a small suite, as hotel bedrooms seldom make good places to relax when one is sitting indoors listening to the rain beating against the windows. They are, however usually heated.

You might be best suited by bed and breakfast, or demi-pension terms, but the business of eating out does raise the cost of living more than somewhat, except in Greece where local tavernas are astonishingly cheap, even if the cuisine is not exactly *soignée*. There is the fact that in many holiday areas most of the restaurants close down in winter, and the rest have less extensive menus which means you can end up with the same thing every night. Self-catering hotels are rare. Nevertheless there are people who maintain that this option is an economical version of the boat/villa scenario.

Laying up the boat

If you are going to move ashore for the winter, go home or go off into the wilds of interior Europe, it will be necessary to lay up the boat. The safest place to lay up is in a purpose-built marina where a good agency is available to keep an eye on the boat. She will generally be safe enough in her berth, the main risk being theft of equipment. The market for stolen electronic equipment along the Riviera and the south coast of Britain is extensive.

The winter is also the busy time for those thieves who do not bother with detail, but take the whole boat. These choose their boat with care, take it from its marina mooring at a quiet time, and deliver it to the prospective buyer, who may well have chosen it himself. We have a deep suspicion that some shady yacht-brokers are not above a bit of crookery.

We once watched two overalled workmen doing jobs aboard a German-owned Amel yacht moored next to us in Antibes one autumn. One day they moved her away, and we assumed she had been taken round to the boatyard for hauling out, a common event. Later we heard that a friend of the owner, visiting another country, recognised the boat in which he had so often sailed, and went down to greet his friend. He saw strangers on board, and had the sense to keep away and to telephone the owner, whom he found in Munich. No, no-one had permission to use the boat. The police were told, and they arrested it, together with the thieves. It transpired that the thieves had already negotiated a full season's charters for the stolen yacht in the West Indies. Large marinas such as Antibes, where there is always a good bit of coming and going, can never be secure in winter.

Thieves generally steal good quality production yachts that are difficult to differentiate one from another at first sight, and thus to identify. There is an active market for these. One-offs or personally adapted yachts are seldom stolen. Thieves also steal registration certificates if they can; there is a widespread but erroneous belief that possession of one of these constitutes evidence of ownership.

The south of France and northern Italy are now well away from the attractive cruising grounds. That is to say that these waters would be attractive, and obviously once were when cruised by far fewer boats, and before the invention of huge high-powered speedboats which have recently come out of the woodwork. These 60 footers, which can do 50 knots in calm weather, have extended the nausea radius by hundreds of miles to areas where one could previously cruise for weeks in joyous peace, completely untroubled by the intrusive jet ski. Good Heavens! we used to think water-skiing was bad enough; what instrument of the devil conceived the jet ski? May his toe nails grow inward.

In Greece there are not many marinas, and long may it continue, since the anchorages are among the most beautiful you could find. For the time being the only genuine marinas are near Athens and are subject to the same problems as the French ones, not excluding the thieving.

There are marinas in Turkey, usually well-managed and pleasant, but rather expensive. Many people leave their boats there successfully, and enjoy their stay.

Outside marinas the prospect for laying up safely in winter is limited. Often a better deal is to have the boat laid up ashore, where supervision is more reliable. There are various agencies in various ports (some only partly sheltered), which will undertake care of a laid up boat. These agencies are numerous, and so are the complaints about them. This is not surprising, for the agents offer a complex service; one could expect that now and then the *Skylark* will find they have *Daisybelle's* laundered cushion covers when they move aboard in spring, but sadly many of the complaints are worse than that.

At the moment there are too many enterprises trying to look after laid-up yachts on a shoestring and with no reserves to cope with problems as they arise. Those of us who stay for the winter see just what happens to these boats when their owners are not there. There is, of course, no regulation of this minor industry: *caveat emptor*.

One of the chief joys of cruising is in visiting new places. If the set-up you organise involves laying-up always in the same port, close to your cottage, perhaps, then the tendency is to cruise that area every year, or at most to make short forays into the immediately adjacent. This leaves some lovely areas of the world unvisited.

In our discussions with other cruising folk we have often heard wistful longings to visit other parts that have been shelved because the owners lack the physical or nautical resources to cross oceans, or perhaps the self-confidence. It also has to be said that the ocean crossing boat has to be designed and kept to a higher standard, and is more suited to the folk who would live aboard all the year round.

Shipping your boat
Some people ship their boat as deck cargo from say, Europe to Miami or vice versa. This is often not as expensive as it sounds, but it does involve some organisation at each end. No firm advice can be given because circumstances change continuously; often the successful shipping is the result of a chance opportunity rather than a carefully planned event. We have not heard of many actually doing this, but there are many who would like to. One Dutchman, the author Jan de Hartog, shipped a Dutch barge over as deck cargo and cruised (and wrote about) the Intracoastal Waterway. That would have been quite an enterprise, but he was in the Dutch merchant marine, so he could

have been expected to have good knowledge of ways and means.

We have conceived the notion of having a cruising boat which would fit inside a standard large container, like a ship in a bottle. The idea would be to own one's own specially-fitted container which would be a store for various items while the boat is in use.

Shipping the boat in its container from port A to port B would be comparatively easy. Its delivery to the port by truck would present no problems, its loading on board a container ship would be routine, and the same at the port of arrival. If one wished to finish the cruise at a different port to the one where you started, then the container could be shipped empty, or even with your car or reserve gear in it. You would probably have an arrangement with a professional cargo agent who would see to the formalities for you.

As a bonus, while the boat is not in use it would be in very secure weatherproof stowage.

But, you reasonably say, would the boat not be rather narrow? Yes, is the reply, but we point out that 2 m 30 cm is broader than the four berth yacht in which we made our first ever Med cruise in 1954. She can be longer, which gives her some potential speed, and provides some stowage, and bear in mind that in tropical or Med-summer climes one does a lot of one's living on deck. The boat we envisage would have a large cockpit, well fitted and shaded for such living. We know of no-one doing this at the moment, but would be prepared to discuss the project with any interested parties.

There is a potential snag to this scheme. This is that a boat arriving in a foreign country as cargo is sometimes treated differently, and less conveniently, than a boat arriving on its own bottom. There is need of some collected data on this subject, but that is difficult because the Customs authorities of many rather disorganised countries are notoriously unwilling to commit themselves to hypothetical verdicts in advance. We think that this method of operating would necessitate establishing a relationship with a professional shipping agent, and always using the same one.

Cruising abroad

Remember that yacht clubs as the British know them do not exist in many places abroad. Even in the colonies or ex-colonies the local yacht clubs are rarely concerned with cruising. Many of them are not really much concerned with yachting in any form. Some have an active small boat racing membership, heavily outnumbered by the social members who tend to dominate the club. A typical scenario would see the dinghy park being reduced in size in order to build another tennis or squash court. And when the social facilities become predominant, the membership usually fills up and one gets the phenomenon of would-be sailors being excluded from membership of a yacht club because there are too many who want to play tennis. Often this situation has come about because the community is too small to support more than one social club, and the yacht club is more successful and sociable than the others. Sometimes it is the other way round. We remember an archery club in Ceylon (now Sri Lanka), the Bandarawela Bow Club, that had no archers, but threw some lovely parties. Nevertheless the combined social and yacht club may suit people who are coming in from outside, always providing there is room for them to join.

In Mediterranean waters yacht clubs are mostly commercial businesses masquerading as clubs. Even in the marinas where there are sometimes clubs for berth-holders the same applies. There are very few clubs as we know them in Britain; most are in effect commercial cafe-bar-restaurants in the management of which the members have very little say.

If you are really attracted by this way of life, and if possessing reasonable assets, think of the West Indies or the Bahamas as a base. The ambience is not so millionaire as people think, and we have always found the people very hospitable. Property, however, can be expensive in some places, but there is no need to live next door to Princess Margaret or Mick Jagger. There are much cheaper and, we think, rather nicer islands. They are also quieter.

It is already apparent that a goodly number of Americans (and a growing number of Europeans, too) retire to Florida to have a small house and a boat, and not all of these are luxury affairs. The whole Intracoastal Waterway area in Florida is based on the concept of the waterside residence with mooring, and square miles of swamp have been drained to make side canals lined with villas. There are thousands of boats and waterside properties there, probably more than in the whole of Europe put together, not excluding Holland. Florida is oriented to two social groups: the Latino-Caribbean immigrants, and the retired. While the former make a lot of noise, both politically and physically, the latter bring enormous wealth to the state and are, for America, very well catered for. Most yacht clubs in America are like those in the UK, rather than the commercial affairs of the Med, though they are often multi-function clubs. Like many things in America, they tend to be bigger, glossier and more expensive than those in Britain, but there are exceptions.

You would have to seek out your preferred type: there are some super ones in the Chesapeake, for example, but that is getting north and very cold in winter. Even the northern part of Florida can get cold, and we once cruised through Georgia with ice on our decks (we must have been mad!).

The Flying Dutchman, en route about 350 years ago from Batavia round the Cape of Good Hope, was guilty of blasphemy in a storm. His ship is doomed to sail until he is redeemed by the love of a good woman. Every seven years he is allowed to come ashore and look for one.

At home or abroad, short distance cruising is in some ways the best of both worlds. You have your house to be comfortable in, you can choose when to go cruising and take advantage of the deep peace of out-of-season voyaging, and if there is any little problem, you can stop the cruise and go home.

In considering choice of boat for this type of cruising one should look at Chapter 9 on long-term cruising, because in many cases one is in a boat long enough for it to need many of the refinements and comforts that are needed in a home. One difference is that you will not go on so long as a rule, nor will you be making ocean passages. By limiting your cruising ground you will have a better chance of avoiding bad weather, though the boat should have some such capability for safety's sake.

Another difference is that you will not have to carry nearly so much gear. Winter clothes take up a lot of space for a start, and you will probably not want to take all your hobby equipment with you. Nor all your books. Because you will be on board generally over the summer period the heating requirements will be less, and simpler arrangements for washing and showering are acceptable. The result will be a smaller boat.

Smaller boats mean easier berthing, but you must resist the temptation to do much in the way of pulling and pushing your boat about by main force. We still believe it is worth having a powered anchor windlass and a self-stowing anchor, if the anchor is over 25 lbs and the cable is all chain.

But with boats under 35 feet (10.7 m) or thereabouts the practice of mooring bows-to the quay in the Med is much more advisable. We discuss this in Chapter 11.

We would not worry too much about the accommodation in boats of this type. A production boat is probably going to suit quite well, and the best advice would be to keep things fairly simple. And yet you may be on board for several months – she must be comfortable.

It is impossible to say that this manufacturer's boats are or are not suitable, for most offer a range. The best thing to do might be to read our comments on the good things for a live-aboard boat and to discard those that are clearly meant to involve the creation of a home that can go deep sea. There is a wide choice, but *in general* the American and British boats rate fairly well under this heading, followed by the Dutch. The Scandinavians are mostly too ritzy and offer poor value for money, while one or two of the French factory yachts might creep into consideration if one was very tolerant. They are mostly lightweight and built very cheaply, and thus offer a usable boat for not very much money.

Very many of the retired people we meet cruising have found a fifty-

fifty solution, a season cruising and the winter ashore, very satisfactory. Some even go back to their old homes, in London, Berlin, Paris, Toronto, wherever, for a taste of the bright lights and some family life. There is a lot to be said for it.

7

Chartering: A Trouble-free Option?

Au clair de la lune, ami Bénéteau,
Prêtez-moi un bateau pour naviguer les flots

Tired of bricks and mortar, time to have a break;
Let's have a mug of porter, and go, for Heaven's sake!

I T WOULD BE WRONG to cover the possibilities of sailing for the retired without mentioning chartering. This gives the yachtsman the opportunity to sail without the chore of maintaining the boat.

There are four sorts of charter that might be considered:

1   Chartering a largish yacht

This assumes a professional crew who will undertake the sailing, and the catering. At one extreme the charterer will be able to lounge about the deck in a silk dressing-gown, smoking a Balkan Sobranie cigarette in a fifteen-inch holder and pretending to be Noel Coward. At the other he might be on a yacht with a Greek crew where they run a noisy generator that blows black smoky exhaust over the deck at mealtimes to encourage the party to go ashore to eat.

Either sort of charter is expensive, but it involves little or no energy, and if one's ability has declined and one has enough money, it is an effective way of savouring some of the delights of going afloat. The most extreme form is, of course, *chez* Cunard, but here we think one would hardly notice one were afloat at all.

2   Bare-boat chartering

Here the charterers have the use of the boat to do what they will with her without any supervision. The hiring company usually put aboard a parcel of goodies for the newly-arrived crew, take them for a few minutes' trial sail, check the inventory, and then off you go into the wild blue yonder. Generally someone in the party is required to show evidence of competence, a requirement that seems to us to be very leniently enforced. We questioned one hiring party whose boat we had just extricated from a parlous situation. What qualification had they been asked to show? They replied that all the company wanted was a cheque that didn't bounce. Further research shows that this is the norm. Some seagod seems to protect these innocents from harm.

Normally one makes up one's own party, but sometimes hirers-out will have a pot-luck boat for solo charterers. Chartering is not cheap, but many people find it less expensive and less trouble than keeping up their own yacht, especially if they are going to be afloat for less than one month in twelve.

It is this bare-boat charter that one finds on the Broads, or the inland waterways both in Britain or on the continent. We found it much less established in the USA, but it does exist. It is very common in the West Indies. A note of caution: not all hirers-out are conscientious, or even honest, and quite a few of the boats on offer are badly maintained, or badly fitted out. Some have inadequate charts, or even photocopies to navigate by. The hiring company may be late handing them over, or the boat may not be available for you at all, or you may get some alternative boat. (Contracts are all written for the benefit of the hirer-out.)

Good companies are very good, and have much repeat business; the bad companies are truly awful and verge on the fraudulent. There is no effective form of consumer protection out of Britain or the USA. Check that your company is a properly paid-up member of a reputable charterers' association, and that the membership is current, and then check with a body such as the RYA that the charterers' association is reputable. This may sound like paranoia, but we know so many people who have been seen off, and a spoiled holiday can be an expensive disaster. A glossy advertisement and a beguiling brochure are not enough. It has been known for stolen boats to be offered for charter, usually at an enticing rate. You get nothing for nothing; deal only with the good companies, who are not necessarily the biggest. Word of mouth and repeat business is the best recommendation.

At its best this form of sailing provides one with a moderately trouble-free way of cruising in many parts of the world.

3   Flotilla holidays

Here the chartered yacht is part of a small fleet, or flotilla, which cruises in company with a lead boat which will contain a leader (who is supposed to be expert, but interpret that very loosely), an engineer, who will repair most things that go wrong with these very heavily used boats, and a lady called a hostess, or something equivalent, who does odd jobs, usually knows a bit of the language and where to shop, and keeps the leader company.

Some companies are losing the emphasis on cruising, and providing more of a nautical knees-up with everyone eating at the same tavernas, mooring cheek-by-jowl, and getting the same sand in their food at the weekly barbecue. The ones who want to cruise can usually do a week of acclimatisation, and then strike off on their own, knowing that advice is always available on Channel 10, a great comfort if your skills are medium and your knowledge of the yacht and the waters limited. A great many people have a lot of fun this way, and learn as they go. As far as we could discover there is no upper age limit, and if a disability is involved, reputable companies go to great lengths to see that the person has a comfortable and enjoyable time.

4 The instructional charter

In this instance the crew are all there to learn from the (usually) owner-skipper. The associated pains and pleasures vary with the locality and the personality of the skipper. Some skippers are benign old tars who amuse their guests in the dog watches with salty yarns while the oil lamp swings under the skylight, and his wife prepares a gourmet meal. Others feed their prisoners on curried split peas, have them holystoning decks before breakfast, and fall just short of flogging the shirkers. (Come to think of it, this might possibly suit some people – it takes all sorts).

Some skippers make the whole thing so painless and enjoyable that they have the same customers back to perfect their skills and have a good holiday year after year; this strikes us as the perfect recommendation. Given the likely introduction of compulsory licences for yachtsmen (something we are very dubious about), this form of holiday afloat may pay practical dividends as well as being enjoyable. Friends who have done this report very enthusiastically, and wear their RYA Yachtmaster's sweaters with pride.

A caution on chartering in spring

Older people would be advised before chartering bare or flotilla boats early in the season to ask the company searching questions on whether the water tanks have been thoroughly flushed through since the winter lay up. Stagnant tanks can cause pulmonary infections to which older folk are especially vulnerable. We have observed in autumn that these boats are laid up hundreds together in a matter of a few days, and their water tanks may be neglected. See 'Legionnaire's disease' in Chapter 13.

There is another problem connected with hiring for the retired. The charter fleet comes mainly from the French boat factories, probably

...cause the builders are prepared to deal on bulk prices and modify the specification to suit the short expected active life of these boats. They provide much short-term holiday fun for the young, but the builders are no better than any others when considering the needs of the less active. We have seen people of all ages who for various reasons are slow and stiff in the joints fall while boarding or disembarking, or tumbling in the cockpits while berthing, and getting into difficulties jamming their less than agile fingers in the miniaturised microcleats with which these boats are fitted.

We hope, by drawing attention to these matters, to persuade the builders to give them some consideration. We who are not marvellously athletic, for whatever reason, represent quite a good potential market.

On the inland waters, the well-established agencies maintain a strict surveillance over the companies in their 'stables'. One should be able to charter through these agencies, especially Blakes and Hoseasons, without serious problems. Most French inland charter companies are very well run. It is significant that inland charter in Britain is much cheaper than on the continent.

Hiring or chartering is a good way of widening one's experiences when associated with some simple home sailing activity which might cover the major part of one's time. The principal difficulty is usually getting together a compatible party to spread the load, both financial and physical. With congenial friends and relatives, you are made.

8

Consider the Canals

Jack Sprat preferred a Cat,
His wife a Barquentine.
They couldn't agree so they bought one each,
And sailed on the Serpentine.

MANY PEOPLE FEEL that the 60s is a little late in life to learn about the deep ocean, and contemplate canals as an alternative. The idea of wandering, while you still have the wish and ability, in a not too threatening environment, and then quietly subsiding into a back-water to listen to the chuckle of coots and watch the reflections of the play of water on the ceiling of your barge is very appealing. It is attractive to many who feel that the sea and those who sail it are too rough. Some feel that at their age they should not have to cope with flying pots and pans, and risk their possessions being scattered all over the floor. They also want some room to put these possessions.

A barge has an area roughly equivalent to a small flat. It has more space for storage, and these spaces are a more sensible shape than the often triangular lockers in deep sea yachts. There is usually more headroom. The galley is quite as good as anything in a bijou residence on land. There is always a pleasant sitting-out patio, often with pots of flowers, parsley and other garden herbs, even occasionally a potted shrub of quite sizable dimensions. The cat snoozes in the wheelhouse window behind its lace curtain.

We have seen much smaller craft than barges on the canals, which have also been elegant and charming inside and out, with the orna-ments and crystal on display, the brass kettle on the stove, and lace curtains at the windows. If the weather is unkind, these craft are cosy and relaxing places to spend time in, and there are seldom big enough waves in the canals to ruffle the peace inside, or shift the glasses on the sideboard.

Canal and sea reciprocity

Boats designed specifically to be ideal for canal cruising are not suitable for any other type of cruising, though the converse is usually possible: that is to take a sea-going craft into a canal network for a change of scene, provided her dimensions are within the limits of the canal's facilities. Such a calm water passage to the Med for example, can be a pleasant interlude in what could otherwise be a long and often rough voyage. Note that we are discussing inland waterways, not ship canals which are really sea-going short-cuts.

It is also possible to design boats that are suitable for both elements, though even with dual-purpose craft, there is a deliberate change of emphasis and style when changing the mode from open water to canal. Even if the boat itself changes little (except by being temporarily dismasted), the crew change their habits and outlook. For one thing, sailing is not usually possible on canals. In some places it is even forbidden, when to do so might be a danger to navigation. It follows that the motor becomes more important.

Many of the comments that one can make about river or estuary cruising apply also to canals, but estuaries are tidal, and can be rough, while canals are calm, have locks and are usually narrow enough to prevent you from turning round whenever you want to.

What sized boat?

Many British canals are limited to boats that are so narrow that a tall man can barely sleep athwart them. To get a range of comfortable facilities the boat becomes unduly long for its width, and it feels as if one is navigating a brightly-painted exclamation mark. For short periods these are fine, but would need very thoughtful conversion to make a permanent home. There are broad canals, but they constitute a much smaller network, while broader beamed boats on the Broads or the Thames, for example, are more or less confined to these waters. Many people find much happiness on British waterways and further research is worth while if it attracts you. The waterways of Britain need our support if they are to survive.

On most of the Continent the beam (width) can be up to 5 metres, and the draught as much as $1^1/2$ metres, though $1^1/4$ is more convenient as the edges of the canal are shallower. Bridges have a minimum headroom of 3 m 40, enabling craft to have a clearance height, or air-draught as some call it, of about the same figure. Added together these give 4 m 65 overall thus allowing two floors, so to speak.

Be cautious about the 3 m 40. The above dimensions apply only to the canals on the Freycinet standard, and there are many smaller 'narrow gauge' canals, many of them pretty and attractive. The Canal du

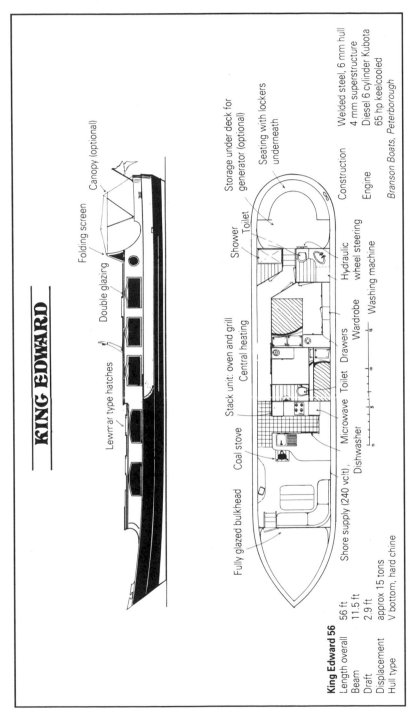

KING EDWARD

Lewmar type hatches

Double glazing

Folding screen

Canopy (optional)

Fully glazed bulkhead

Coal stove

Shore supply (240 volt), Dishwasher

Stack unit: oven and grill
Central heating

Microwave Toilet Drawers

Storage under deck for generator (optional)

Seating with lockers underneath

Shower
Toilet

Wardrobe

Washing machine

Hydraulic wheel steering

King Edward 56

Length overall	56 ft
Beam	11.5 ft
Draft	2.9 ft
Displacement	approx 15 tons
Hull type	V bottom, hard chine

Construction	Welded steel, 6 mm hull
	4 mm superstructure
Engine	Diesel 6 cylinder Kubota
	65 hp keelcooled

Branson Boats, Peterborough

An example of a well thought out British design of broad beam canal craft which would make an attractive home.

Nivernais in France, for example, a lovely canal, has a maximum headroom of only 2 m 70 and 1 m 15 of draught, which makes the double decker a bit less practical. Other canals which quote headroom figures roughly equal to the Freycinet standard (the Canal du Midi, for example) require caution because some of the bridges are virtually ancient monuments; they are arched, and the given headroom applies only to a very narrow portion in the centre.

It is possible to design your boat so that the higher parts are demountable to pass those sections that have low headroom. Traditionally, the demountable parts are the wheelhouse roof and windows.

The larger dimensions possible on the Continent have their counterpoints: the locks are much bigger and the skipper of a smaller boat can find it thrown about rather badly if the lock-keeper lets the water in too fast. If the passing pleasure-boater has interrupted a football match on the TV this is quite likely to happen. In locks it is more comfortable to have a boat of nearly the maximum beam; one is thrown about much less, and only in a fore-and-aft direction.

Boats in general

Canal boats in general have an economic advantage over sea-going craft in that they do not have to be equipped for meeting the dangers of a rough sea. This can be an enormous saving not only in first cost, but also in the annual expenditure to keep safety measures up to scratch. For example the boat can be fitted with household window frames instead of the robust nautical ones (though safety glass or triplex is a commendable precaution on all moving vehicles), and much of the superstructure can be of lighter construction. On the other hand she can expect a lot more bashing about in the locks and when passing commercial barges, as well as in the inevitable groundings, so the hull must be strong. It is worth remembering that most of the damage a sea-going craft sustains during its active lifetime is suffered while manoeuvring in harbour, and a canal boat is in harbour, effectively, all the time. By the same token, in the canals you are driving constantly, as if you were in a car, and an autopilot would be of no use.

Steel is possibly the best material to build in but involves maintenance routines and at our age we want to avoid too much menial work. On the other hand we now have all the time to do it, and steel does not rust in fresh water as badly as it does in salt. It is worth noting that many continental commercial barge owners do not re-paint the under part of a hull at all; they find it cheaper to wait until it corrodes and then renew the bottom, usually after about twenty years. They consider antifouling unnecessary because they run aground so often that they scrape the weed off in the mud, which must be a con-

'GRP boats should be well protected.'

solation to those ecologists who blame the boating community for all
the world's watery ills. Antifouling, it seems, is bad for the dogwhelk.
The death of the dogwhelk would have been greeted by the old fishermen in our home towns with a surly grunt of unrestrained rapture,
since the dogwhelk ruins their nets, and eats their bait. Now it is our
fishermen who are becoming extinct instead of the dogwhelk.
Something has gone wrong somewhere.

Glass-fibre and other construction should ideally be well protected
with an all round fender strake of hard wood capped with a 75 mm x
10 mm thick steel band. Whether you choose steel, glass fibre or wood
as the main material for your hull, the increase in size for the same
expenditure on both first cost and maintenance allows one to have a
much larger boat than a sea-going equivalent. This naturally increases
the comfort, and size is not nearly so important a factor in considering
ease of handling in the canals. In fact too small a boat can be a disadvantage: the steadiness and momentum of a larger boat help in close
quarters manoeuvring near big barges. Slipping barges is no problem if
you go to traditional slips such as those at Conflans, St Jean-de-Losne,
and Arles, where it is cheap. Yacht yards, of course, will suck their
teeth and charge you an arm and a leg.

House-boats

There is, among navigational authorities in any country a strong
antipathy to live-aboards and house-boats. Many have not even bothered to discover the essential difference between these two classes.
House-boat dwellers generally live in boats that stay in one place.
Examples are to be found in Little Venice in central London, where for
the most part the boats are well kept and inoffensive. The Amsterdam
houseboats, thousands of them, are world famous to the extent of
being a tourist attraction, but even in this city there is a scruffy element to be found.

Live-aboards as we define them keep mobile and have no fixed
mooring, at least for most of the year. They have to keep their boats in
good enough condition for safe navigation, and mostly they lead this
life by choice and conviction, so that they are generally at one with
their environment. The responsibilities of safe navigation are con-
ducive to a generally responsible attitude to all things.

Problems connected with house-boat dwelling arise because in
Britain the cost of houses has risen sharply for several decades. This
has brought to our waterways and harbours, colonies of persons who
would prefer normal housing, but cannot afford it. Usually they are
also financially incapable of looking after their boats properly.
Sometimes they have no interest in the finer points of ecology.

France has this problem too; there they call these people *marginales*,
for they are living financially on the margin of society. A small colony
of them moving into a water-borne community can soon destroy any
pleasant amenities that once existed. They often inhabit half-converted
old ships' lifeboats, lighters, and semi-wrecks that are no longer seaworthy, their leaky decks covered with nailed down sheets of plastic, a
sort of floating shanty-town.

The Amsterdam colony already mentioned is mostly 'legal', (boats
that have regularised their position and pay dues) but there exist some
'illegals'. The Dutch, however, have no reason to consider most houseboats as anything but perfectly respectable, since almost all are neat
and well kept. Some are very elaborate: one barge home we saw had a
smaller low barge in front of it on which had been planted lawns,
flower beds and a couple of small trees. One of these, since we passed
on St Nicholas Day, was decorated and lit with fairy lights.

Boats such as these should surely offend nobody, though even in
Holland they have their critics. Here in Britain, it is the flipside of the
attractive and desirable dwellings that upsets the authorities and the
neighbours: the rusty caravan precariously afloat on a few oildrums,
or the rotting hull aground on fifty years of jetsam, three storeys high
and protected from the rain by a flapping tarpaulin old enough to
have wrapped the body of Admiral Benbow.

Can we please appeal to fair-minded authorities to control the excesses without blanket prohibitions of what can be a perfectly reasonable and attractive way of life? We can remember some of the old converted wherries that used to be inhabited by some of Broadland's most lively characters. They looked after their boats and their bankside plots, and they and their predecessors have been for centuries one of the traditional features of riverside life. Long may it continue.

Catamarans

Do not overlook the suitability of multihulls for the Continental canals. Many catamarans have a beam of less than the Freycinet standard of 5.05 metres (trimarans are typically slightly wider than catamarans), and we have mentioned elsewhere that it is desirable to have the beam of one's boat as near the lock-width as conveniently possible to minimise the throwing about when the lock-keeper is a bit too enthusiastic about letting the water in.

Multihulls are usually dual purpose; that is they are both canal and sea-worthy, and this means it can be safer and easier to make short sea or estuary crossings to get into the canals. Their hulls, of course will be more fragile than the purpose built canal boat, though we have seen a purpose-built steel canal catamaran.

Buying or converting your own barge

There are many retired folk passing their time living in converted barges on the Continental canals. These provide cheap homes and the cost of living in France for instance, is very similar to that in Britain. We discuss living afloat in general in a later chapter.

Barges are not always enormous. The Dutch in particular have some very handsome little barges down to about 16 metres length and all sizes upwards. Of course the smaller ones are in demand for private use, so usually fetch a premium, but you would be surprised at how cheap a perfectly good medium sized barge of between 25 and 30 metres is.

If you are looking to buy or convert a barge for your own use whether in England or on the Continent, good sources of information are the French magazine *Fluvial*, and The Journal of the Dutch Barge Association, described later.

Our own experience in buying a commercial barge in Holland, bringing it to Great Yarmouth for the major steel work (Bure Marine Ltd can be recommended) and converting it to a sea-going home has been a rewarding if rather exhausting one. Anyone in their 60s ought to be able to do the detailed fitting out themselves, but there is more to it than that; there is some very heavy work to do and skilled assistance would be required for the basic conversion. It took us five years in all, but we have fitted our barge out for use at sea as well as in the canals; most people reckon on two to three years with a good deal of help.

There is a sizeable barge-loving community in St Jean-de-Losne and in Auxerre, both in France. They are usually approachable people who like talking about barges. A land tour of the canals, chatting to people you meet as you go, is a rewarding and enjoyable preliminary to the way of life.

Bow-thrusters

If converting a barge then we would strongly advise fitting a bow-thruster. Professionals can mostly make their boats sit up and beg, but even so we have seen them make some awful bloomers when manoeuvring in a strong wind. The ability to make the bows move sideways is a great comfort when manoeuvring, and an elderly crew should not have to push and shove a big and unco-operative artefact about by main force. Toy bow-thrusters are a waste of money; one needs to have one with about one quarter of the horse-power of the main engine.

British canals and the narrow boat

We ourselves have very little experience of British canals and that little bit goes back to the days of long ago when commercial barges still plied. But we have cruised the Continental canals and can discuss the pros and cons of canals in a general way. So our comments on the British canals are the result of listening carefully to several people on whose judgement and experience we feel we can rely, and then stirring the pot and filtering to find the salient information.

Once again things are divided into shortish term cruising and living aboard for longer periods, or even permanently. Younger people can organise their holidays by owning a narrow boat which they have use of at agreed times, but which pays for itself by being chartered by the fortnight to the public by a competent yard for the rest of the season, (which can even include Christmas!). This option is probably not so relevant for the retired, for they will usually want longer use of the boat for themselves, nor are they likely to be able to exploit any tax advantages that may arise. It seems to us that retired folk favouring the canals would do well to have their own exclusive craft. Narrow boats are not expensive in comparison with sea-going craft, nor is their maintenance nearly such a problem.

There are enough waterways in Britain to give many days and miles of contented navigation, and they extend into both the north and south of the country. There are too, some parts of the canal system which are isolated from the rest, and because the boats are narrow it is possible to transport the shorter ones by road to enjoy for a time such disconnected waterways as the Broads or the Scottish canals.

If it is advisable to have a home base as well, you will want to discuss with the yard that builds your new boat, or sells you a ready made one, whether they undertake maintenance for clients, and look after the vessels if they are not in use. There are several builders of repute, but some of the best work is achieved, we think, where the accommodation is finished by specialists who do not necessarily make the actual hulls. This is a growing tendency in all boat-building for the 'finishing trades' are much more difficult to organise profitably, and it is all best left to those specialists who have solved the problems.

Other Countries' systems

Waterways in Europe
Given the improved communications with the continent, it seems to us that anyone interested in canal cruising, especially those living towards the south of England, might look to the French, Belgian and Dutch systems for their pleasures.

Another reason why these might appeal in particular to older folk is that in Britain most of the locks on our inland water system are operated by the boat's crew without any help at all, either mechanical or manual. Too much of this imposes a strain on people who are past their prime and risking hernias or subject to arterio-sclerotic risks. On the continent, where at present there is still commercial traffic (though it diminishes yearly in some parts) the locks are operated either by a lock-keeper, or remote controlled machinery.

There is of course a moral obligation of politeness to 'help' the lock-keeper, if only by chatting to pass the time. If you can take a hand at winding it expedites the passage, for otherwise you would have to wait while the lock-keeper walked twice the length of a long lock between opening one gate and its partner. The lock-keeper is often female, for it is not a well-paid job and usually her man goes out to work elsewhere, leaving his wife to operate the lock during working hours, which, paradoxically is probably heavier work than that of her spouse. We have met lock-keepers of both sexes who have earned themselves occupational hernias (Laurel has a facility for bringing out the strangest confidences in people she has only just met). We should reassure you that Lock-keeper's Hernia is typically induced by efforts to keep the systems free of ice and flood debris in winter, and is not generally due to winding the handles that work the gates. This can be just a nice workout if you don't have to do it seventeen times between dawn and dusk. This number sticks in our mind as being the most locks we ever did in one day, much against our will we assure you, but we were being hustled out of a long length of canal that was going to be emptied, and if we were not to end up marooned on the muddy bed of the dried-up canal for a month we had to do as we were told. Life is like that sometimes. Canals expose you to rather more bureaucratic botheration than the sea.

Belgium

The Belgian system is small, and therefore has to be thought of as an intermediate between the larger systems of France, Holland and Germany. It is not well maintained and it is appallingly polluted, but it does pass through or round some very beautiful old towns.

Holland

The Dutch system is superb. There are those with much greater knowledge of Dutch canals than ours but we can say that we found the other *binnenvaart* (inland waterways) users hospitable and polite, the lock-keepers quietly efficient, and the whole set-up thoroughly enjoyable. The only drawbacks we can find are that it is so pleasant to cruise that almost all the Dutch, and a good number of other Europeans are out there cruising it. This means that it can occasionally be difficult to find a convenient mooring.

Germany

The German system is not known to us personally. We have friends who have cruised it extensively, and who say that it is very well organised, and that the other users and officials are hospitable and helpful. As you would expect, the rules are meant for keeping. In Germany they do not understand that the British find it commendable that Nelson put his telescope to his blind eye so that he could not see his superior's signal. They would have shot him. So might we, if he'd lost.

The Baltic

The German system connects with other East European systems. These are mostly river navigations but we imagine they could make interesting diversions so that there is no reason why a canal cruiser on the continent need consider himself hemmed in. If one's boat is even half sea-worthy one could choose the right weather and make the short trip over the Baltic and try the lovely Swedish canal to Stockholm.

The old Red Block

What about further East? While we were in France the Berlin Wall fell, and a group of young and enthusiastic French bought a 38 metre *péniche*, (cargo barge), painted her in rainbow colours and set off in a mass of media coverage to navigate on a good-will journey to Leningrad. In the end they could not make it, which supposes a lack of preliminary homework, and they had to do the last stages to Leningrad on the deck of a freighter, which must have been an exciting enterprise.

The Rhine-Danube connection via Austria and the Balkans down to the Black Sea will be a fine journey when the Yugoslavians have stopped fighting each other (and anyone else who gets in their way). For the time being the short passage through the inland waters of that ex-country is inadvisable.

When it is safe once more, the route down the Danube to the Black Sea will make a good alternative to that through the French Canals, especially for those bound ultimately to the eastern Mediterranean. We must hope too, that the old canals to Petrograd, St Petersburg, or whatever Leningrad is called this week will re-open, making it possible to navigate between the Black Sea and the Baltic, across Russia via Moscow and the River Volga. Already a yachting journalist has won a prestigious award from the Ocean Cruising Club (rather out of their element) by a passage from the White Sea to the Black Sea.

The USA and Canada

The Intracoastal Waterway on the other side of the Atlantic, extends from Long Island Sound to the Florida keys, round and through Florida to the Mexican border; there are thousands of miles of sheltered navigation down the East and South coasts of the States. It is part canal, part river, and part sheltered estuary, and the eastern section is an ideal cruising ground. The difficulty for the European lies in crossing the Atlantic to get there, but it is not insurmountable. We did it the hard way, sailing over in our ketch *Fare Well*, but with the right boat it was not all that hard.

It is not that expensive to have a boat shipped over, though because of the different regulations that apply to boats shipped as freight, compared with those that arrive on their own bottoms, it might be advisable to ship one's boat to the Bahamas in order to arrive under one's own steam in the USA so as to be eligible for a cruising permit as a visiting boat, rather than as an import. The USA has very restrictive legislation about boat imports, probably the most restrictive in the world. One could consider buying an American boat over there (that is after all, the object of their restrictive legislation). American builders make hundreds of very good ones (and a few nautical horrors, too, it must be said), and there is a very active second-hand market.

The Intracoastal Waterway is reputed to have been started by George Washington in order to be able to trade along the east coast while the Royal Navy, which in those days was rather bigger than the

USN, was very effectively keeping up a blockade. The waterway extends in various forms from Cape Cod down to the Mexican Border, and one really does see America at its best. Wherever you go in the world, the country-folk always seem to be the nicest, and we met some fine people down the waterway.

There are other inland waterways in America. The Mississippi River complex, the Hudson River and canal up to the Lakes, and in Canada there is the mighty St Lawrence going up to the Great Lakes. We have noted that they are navigable, and that folk do enjoy themselves there.

Other parts of the world

In theory it would be possible to have a boat suitable for inland waters and ship it to other places where there are big rivers or canals. We have brief experience of some of these: The River Li at Gue Lin in China, the Hooghly in India, among others; it is possible to cruise them and we would enjoy going again. The problem in some of these countries would be to overcome the bureaucracy and get the necessary permits. A young friend of ours took his own small Wayfarer up the Nile. It was a fascinating trip by all accounts, but he very nearly gave up the attempt in despair. The Egyptians, desperate for tourism, nevertheless put so many bureaucratic obstacles in his way that a less indomitable spirit would have given up.

Coping on waterways

Judging by the wide variety of craft seen on the canal systems, almost anything goes, but some have features that commend themselves especially to the more senior among us. In our experience the only daily activities which would trouble the less fit would be managing the locks, and boarding or leaving the boat, which is much the same problem in effect, and the perennial problem of lifting things.

Locks

Typically, a Continental canal lock has a rise or fall of between two and three metres. If one is to assist the lock-keeper, (in manual locks this is more or less obligatory), or make fast unaided in an automatic lock (and it would be unwise to pass through a lock without making fast securely), then at one end or the other of the operation, you will have to climb up or down the lock wall to or from your boat.

One can avoid this when going downhill by making fast with doubled lines that can be slipped from inboard after the boat has dropped in the lock. Coming into an empty lock that is un-manned and without rising (floating) bollards, the situation is different. Now, there is little option but to scramble up a weedy and slippery vertical ladder that is let into the lock wall. It will also lack a stanchion at the top to help you over the most difficult bit; all-in-all, quite a hazardous way of getting a rope on a bollard.

So a desirable feature here would be an accessible wheelhouse roof or similar, extending, either permanently or temporarily, well out to the side of the vessel so that you could step out on to the lockside with little effort. A minor scramble, perhaps. But watch out for arched bridge and tunnel limitations; perhaps a removable upper gangway would be best on those canals where the bridges or tunnels are arched. Some boats use a portable ladder, but this has its own dangers until the boat is made fast.

Getting ashore

This can be very difficult away from designated berths because it is sometimes impossible to get the boat near the bank where there is not sufficient depth of water. Commercial barges on the Continent have a hinged pole, about 6 m long, supported on a wire topping lift. This is normally stowed alongside the barge, but when Madame wishes to go shopping she perches herself on the end of this pole which is then swung out over the water and she drops neatly off onto the bank. You can see quite old ladies nimbly leaping on or off these poles, even when the barge is still moving, but they have probably been doing it

'The natural harmonic of the plank ...'

since they could walk; it is second nature. It is a bit late to start now unless you are exceptionally athletic. Laurel categorically refused to undertake this enterprise, even though Bill offered to equip the end of the spar with a chair. 'A ducking stool?' she said with some asperity.

Barges also carry a very long plank gangway, usually a 5 metre length of 300 mm x 30 mm, and this is just long enough to reach the shore when moored. It cannot really be any stronger because it must be light enough to man-handle, and this means that it droops alarmingly, even under the weight of quite a thin person. Worse still, if you are not careful, your steps pick up the natural harmonic of the plank and you bounce up and down like a clown on a trampoline until you learn how to break step. Even an unwary dog ends up providing much innocent amusement to the onlookers.

Such a device is unlikely to appeal to the elderly novice. It is necessary for those vessels which cannot approach the shallow banks (and most canal edges are shallow) because of their draught. Its use could be avoided by constructing canal pleasure craft with a V sectioned bottom with rounded bilges, unfortunately a more expensive construction than the typical flat bottom, squarish bilge.

Getting weights into or out of the boat

As always, we counsel having some means of hoisting on board heavy weights or awkward bundles. Some barges have hydraulic cranes such as are fitted to delivery trucks. In a good sized boat these make a lot of sense. They can also be used for loading/unloading a small motor car (most commercial barges carry a car) which can provide the means of touring the surrounding countryside. You do not need a very large barge to be able to carry a baby car. We carried an old Fiat 500 on our 26 metre *Hosanna* at one time. It lasted well until some French vandals pushed it into the river Rhône.

Weather, heating, and cooling

Summer weather is generally better on the Continent than in the UK, and so, often, is the weather in spring and autumn. But this scarcely applies to winter, when in general France and Belgium have as much rain as the south-eastern side of Britain, and much lower temperatures too. It is a question of having a Continental climate, rather than an oceanic one like Britain's.

For example, Brittany, which sticks out into the Atlantic, is an exception; it has warmish wet winters with westerly winds. The Midi (the extreme South of France) is also an exception, but even there the weather can get cold and very windy in winter. It should be borne in mind that 90% of the French canal system is in the colder parts of France, either in the Northern *départements* or the high central plateau. Where the north-south canal routes cross the high middle of France, over the Mediterranean/English Channel watershed, the canals often freeze in winter. Even down south, where we have spent several winters in the canals within five kilometres of the Mediterranean coast, we have not had a winter without an occasional frost, and in early 1992 there was two feet of snow along parts of the Med coast.

So if looking to live aboard all the year make sure your heating is efficient and that there is a back-up system too, even if you head for the Canal du Midi in the south of France. A friend of ours who lives in a canal barge which he moors for the winter in the Vosges, says that they sometimes have to go shopping on skis. Tristan Jones's account of his journey down the Danube brings home the rigorous winters of Middle Europe, when his cabin was sometimes 26 degrees below zero. The French west coast, which includes the Britanny canals and the western end of the Canal du Midi, down the Garonne to Bordeaux, often has higher temperatures in winter than the fabled Côte d'Azur, but rather less sunshine. Biarritz was once a very fashionable resort. But the west coast is undoubtedly wetter than the south-east.

The Intracoastal Waterway in the United States is also cold in winter, and if you do not want your boat to be frozen in for the winter months you should start south from the New England States in October at the latest. You will need your heating all the way down to Florida.

So where on the European canal system does it get hot, you may ask? Paris can be sweltering in August, and most of France is warm in summer. In the Midi you will get desert heat and parching sunshine. You will want shady awnings, deckspace to laze on, something to produce cold drinks, and some way of cooling yourself down, since few canals are tempting to swim in, even if it were allowed. You will be glad of mosquito screens.

Canal Costs and Dues

Usually, navigation on Continental canals will be cheaper than on British ones. In Britain, the pleasure boat is virtually the only canal user and the British Waterways Board or other navigation authority can and do squeeze the users as they like. One of the biggest expenses incurred will be the annual dues to the Canal Authority, whatever the current government calls it. The British authorities, (particularly the one for the Broads) are inclined to be inflexible and intolerant of any view but their own, particularly regarding houseboats, but in general they succeed in keeping the navigation going against long odds.

Belgium

Travel on the Belgian canals is still virtually free. The Authorities attempted to introduce tolls for pleasure craft in 1991 but the plan was badly conceived and had to be withdrawn. We expect the Belgians will have another shot at introducing a toll before long, especially when they see how the French have done it. In the meantime one has to pay a purely nominal amount at certain locks, an amount so small that it can hardly be worth collecting and accounting for.

France

Until now, navigation has been free on French canals, but the French, who are inclined to be careful and deliberate about their bureaucracy, have been gestating a scheme of charges for some years. Its introduction was postponed with the partial decentralisation and change of constitution of the navigational authority, now Voies Navigables de France or VNF. Though canal dues were confidently announced for 1992 we made a short trip through the Canal du Rhône à Sète into the Rhône itself in February 1992, and came across no French *fonctionnaire* with his hand out. Then came an announcement that all boats were to be charged for the use of the canal system. The administrative tortoise was moving and later that year a new toll was introduced based on the nominal area of water occupied by the boat. See Appendix 2 for details.

A row is brewing about the amount of the charge, but will probably not make much difference. The charge seems to us to be not unreasonable, given the extent of the network and the beautiful country it goes through. Someone has to pay for it all. In the summer of 1992, boats began to come down the canals with the square sticker on their windscreen, indicating that dues had been paid.

Mooring fees would be on top of this, but there are a great number of free temporary moorings, and apart from a winter lay-up one should be able to pass most of the time at free or low-cost moorings.

Holland

On our last passage (in winter) through the Dutch canals from Friesland to the Belgian border we were not charged anything at all.

To set against the lower charges for canal navigation on the Continent will be the cost of crossing the English Channel unless the boat is one's principal home. In the case of retired persons this should be ameliorated by the fact that they now have the leisure to visit their boats for longer periods, the whole summer perhaps, and even then avoid travelling at peak times. Frequent users of the car ferries can get special terms; we expect the same will apply to Eurotunnel. Very good reductions are available if you buy your rail or air tickets in France, since your respectable age entitles you to airfare reductions and the *Carte Vermeil*, worth having if you travel by rail a lot. In 1992, this was available in France from age 60, but in Britain one had to wait until 65.

Papers and Documents

Vat

One thing to watch out for if buying a commercial barge is to check the VAT position; it may change when converted to a pleasure boat.

Qualifications

So far as we can find out, and we have tried to get definitive rulings with little success, the certificates awarded to Britons by the RYA and which are based on examination containing a practical element are generally satisfactory if in a British flag ship. This whole area is in a state of imminent change; consult the RYA if in any doubt. They won't know either. On British waterways no certificate of competence is required, the 'licence' being merely a form of usage tax.

At present in France no certificate of competence is necessary for foreigners driving foreign flag boats, unless you are carrying passengers. Now some sort of driving licence is under consideration.

The German section requires the skipper to have a certificate of competence: check on this before going.

Insurance and regulations

It will be necessary to have third party insurance, even if you make the decision to cover the hull's risks yourself.

On the French canals insurance is cheaper than for sea-going boats, but not if you insure with British Companies who seem to believe that all hell breaks loose as soon as you pass Calais going south. There is a potential for damage of course because you will be at closer quarters with other boats, but lack of experience by British underwriters causes them to exaggerate the risk. There are excellent Continental insurers who will underwrite the risks willingly for far less. Probably the converse applies in its context. If planning to stay in the canal systems, insure with a specialist company in that medium. It has to be said that the average British or American insurance underwriter or broker knows little about the canals of Europe.

One important factor to be taken into account is that every country has different regulations and the EEC has been ineffective in budging the entrenched prejudices of any of them. This not only applies to financial matters, but also to some extent to signals. It certainly applies to qualifications of skippers. For foreigners a minor disadvantage of the very efficiency of the Dutch involves control by a firm and very authoritarian supervisory body which enforces its rules. Ninety-nine per cent of these rules are eminently sensible, and the rest would be for their own nationals, but we cannot help feeling that, for example, the obligation for foreigners to carry on board the current year's handbook of regulations in the original Dutch is a bit silly. This rule is firmly enforced. Mostly the Dutch are very aware that their language is little known among foreigners; they, themselves are almost universally bi-, or even tri-lingual, and this unbendable rule is a rare example of a shortage of common sense. We wish the examples were equally rare in other canal administrations, including our own.

Magazines

There are magazines devoted to canal cruising, and they also have waterside properties and houseboats advertised in them. In England there is *Waterways World*, and *The Blue Flag*, the Dutch Barge Association's Journal, while in France the magazine *Fluvial* has a column in English contributed by an English girl, Maggy Armstrong who works as mate on a commercial barge. (There! Who says the French are chauvinists. Name any British boating magazine with a regular column in French).

Fluvial has pages of canal craft on offer in all sizes and states of build or conversion. Even if you cannot read French it is still worth examining. The best agents are either Dutch or German, who speak excellent English, even on the telephone, and are used to dealing with English-speaking clients. You will also find this and much other useful information in the DBA's Journal *The Blue Flag*. They report over 700 Dutch barge conversions at present in British ownership.

Both these magazines will contain offers of boats available, for hire as well as for sale, so before committing yourself remember the possibility of hiring a boat on either system for a self-drive holiday, and the same agency, Hoseason's of Oulton Broad, near Lowestoft, can fix up boating holidays in a variety of different countries. This way you can test the water with the toe before diving in.

For anyone interested in learning more about canals, Hugh McKnight has an excellent mail-order bookshop specialising in books about inland waters the world over. (Address in Appendix 3).

The Snags

Are there any drawbacks? If there are, they are more to do with the mooring than the boat. Your belongings may not stay in place quite the way you think they should if you moor in a narrow spot where big commercial barges speed through, sucking the water as they go and you with it. A few experiences like that teach you to moor in wider channels, and to fasten your ropes tautly and with greater care. The boat may sometimes find itself in a little oasis of peace in an industrial desert, where it is miles to the bakery, there are no buses, and dust from the cementworks is blowing on to your geraniums. The cat can stray, unless confined. Worse, it can bring you unwelcome visitors:

'Pussy cat pussy cat, you've been ashore,
You haven't been seen for an hour or more,
Where did you go and what did you catch?'
'My mouse just escaped down the engine room hatch.'

Your canal mooring, though safe from weather, wind and waves, may be subject to worse predators in the shape of thieves and vandals, especially in towns. We have found this to be more of a problem on canals than in harbours and anchorages at sea. The canals often pass, in towns, through the sort of district where you do not want to walk at night, the quays are frequented by unsavoury persons, and precautions should be taken to guard your boat, and lock up your bicycles. (Geraniums are not often stolen). All French riverboats have a built-in Alsatian (we mean the dog, not a native of Alsace) to keep unwanted boarders at bay.

A Cautionary Tale: ('I'm glad I'm not young any more' dept). A man and his wife and daughter were travelling in their pleasure barge down the river Saône and came to the town of Gray. They moored the boat, and the women went to do the shopping and left their man (we will call him Piet) sitting on a park bench. He was not there on their return, but not till night fell did their anxiety send them to the police. They gave his description, name and age, and the whereabouts of the bench where they had last seen him. They were asked if he were in good health, to which they answered yes. 'Then,' said the policeman, 'Do not worry. Look for him on the bench tomorrow.' Piet did not appear the next day. 'Then,' said the policeman, 'He will be back in one week.'

It was indeed a week later that Piet stumbled down onto the deck of the barge to a barrage of questions. He seemed dazed, and was unable to tell them much. He had an impression of lying in bed with white clad figures bending over him saying 'You'll be all right now'. He now complained of a sore patch on his belly, and when the women put him to bed they found a dressing there, but did not wish to disturb it. When after a day or so Piet's head seemed to clear, they moved on. His womenfolk urged him to see a doctor in case the dressing needed changing, and this he did. After the doctor had made his examination he said: 'For no medical reason that I can discern, one of your kidneys has been removed.'

Piet's friend Gilbert, skipper of another pleasure barge, had seen the scar, and told us the story. 'But whether the rest is true, my friends; who knows?' Gray is not far from the Swiss border. A fresh kidney, if of the type required, is worth kidneynapping. Piet would have reappeared in 24 hours if the tissues did not match, or he was not healthy enough. If he had been a pensioner, he would not have been taken at all. One less thing to worry about.

we met several barges owned and skippered by widows and single dames. One pretty little barge had the charming name of *The Contented Woman*. The barge's career had been successfully continued after the death of her husband by a woman who, thinking at first that it was a man's world, took over in some trepidation. Of course, she soon found herself perfectly capable.

To sum up

What are the principal features of canal cruising? Well, one does not get sea-sick for a start, and that has been a deciding factor for a lot of couples we know, where one of the partners either has suffered or thinks they would suffer at sea. Others believe it is an easier form of cruising, doddling along at three miles an hour; why, they can even imagine the horse! Then there is the thought that you do not have to plug on and on into worsening weather and sea in order to get some very moderately comfortable port for the night; a port so moderately comfortable that the swell rolls in and all the boats are banging into each other.

There are moments when these thoughts are justified. One can come across some delightful secluded pub or *auberge* with a terrace leading down to a convenient mooring, a provision shop nearby, and a fresh-water tap to top up your tanks. Interesting passers-by on the bank, and no heavy barges passing to tear your mooring stakes out by the roots.

But do not be deceived into thinking that canal cruising is the easy option. It can be very hard work. To start with one must steer all the time; there is no opportunity to use an autopilot. This requires far more attention than steering at sea, it is more like driving a car with no brakes. There are locks to negotiate, other craft to pass, and big commercial barges can be frightening even if you are experienced.

Then there is almost always a marked shortage of good moorings. Most of those in the guide books are silted up. The canal banks are shallow and can barely be approached, and anyway most of the mooring bitts or rings have long ago been pulled out and never replaced. Much of the canal system in any country either passes through deserted countryside with neither pub, shop, or even telephone, or else runs between large factories belching fumes while loading huge barges with chemicals. And that nice restaurant mentioned in the Michelin Guide has changed hands and now serves plastic fast food.

Between the extremes the main body of truth lies, waiting to be discovered. We prefer sea cruising, but we are able to enjoy the canals too, and we suggest that is a reasonably healthy attitude, one that is shared by many of our friends. Nobody refers slightingly to ditch-crawlers in our hearing: ditch-crawling is skilful work.

PART THREE

Deeper Waters

9

Long-term Cruising

Rubadubdee
Two souls went to sea,
Not far, always gently (they weren't in their prime)
They rounded the world, one small step at a time.

Living aboard your boat while cruising
Those readers who know our sailing history will be aware of our long-standing devotion to living all the year round aboard our very mobile boat. In our middle sixties we are still enjoying this way of life and would recommend it to anyone with our own capabilities and tastes. It is not a way that requires a huge bank balance or any great skills; the old shellbacks of times past were no great geniuses, but they had experience and knew their craft. Anyone ought, one would think, to be able to get by as they did, and learn as they go along.

The idea is beguiling up to a point. If one considers a person at retirement age with his wits about him, there is no real reason why he or she should not become a competent deep-sea cruising yachtsman in a fairly short period, but this must suppose that he is fit enough to recover from his mistakes. For he will make them, come what may, and sailors expend more energy recovering from their misjudgements than in any other activity. And it is the Three Big Mistakes, coming together, one after another, that will probably end our seagoing life.

Given that our energies and stamina decrease with age, and our learning processes start to slow down, it is evident that there will come an age when it would no longer be prudent to start from scratch the process of becoming a proficient off-shore sailor. What that age is must depend on so many personal variables that one cannot be dogmatic about it.

A person with a sailing background who can manage a yacht in home waters will have little problem, (though like all of us he will have plenty of little problems), even if he is used only to comparatively sheltered waters. He or she whose experience is very limited or non-existent would do well to consider whether they will be able to cope. All should take steps to improve skills already acquired.

When we had young children, we worried about them. When they hurt themselves out playing we felt guilty, but children do not learn by being kept in cotton-wool. As a seven year old newly home from two and a half years in orthopaedic hospital, Laurel was immensely grateful to her parents for letting her run wild in summer with the other children, since she now realises how hard they must have found it not to interfere. The children climbed mountains of bricks and swarmed up scaffolding on building sites, leapt off the sea wall on to sand that was never as soft as it looked, played ghosts in an empty house, climbing up to the roof of an outhouse and through the first floor lavatory window. Laurel learnt to ride someone's bike, and eventually fell off it in the High Street, without too much damage. Her parents must have felt as guilty as she did years later, when our own toddler caught her heel in the spokes of a friend's bike.

When our own children grew older, there was plenty more to worry about. Drugs. Motor-bikes. Hitch-hiking. Dubious friends. The Commune phase. Children are given their heads at eighteen, and whether they lose them, keep them, or smash them, is their business, they will tell you. We are doing what we want. Don't worry, Mum. Our children reached adulthood only slightly scathed, and there followed a period of many years when we almost ceased to worry about them. We detect signs that they are beginning to worry about us.

It's unbearable to think of them worrying. We know what it's like to worry about our parents. All those long years of cruising when we would step ashore and phone up our eighty-year-olds (plus) at home: 'Yes, we've arrived safely, but are *you* all right?' The wash of relief to hear 'Yes, my dears, we're fine.' Only later do you tell them how you came through a hurricane, and they happen to mention that Linet broke a wrist picking blackberries for preserving.

At this point the worry is tempered with respect. Why should not the old lady carry on bottling her garden produce as she has always done? She it was, after all, who had a sign up on her kitchen corkboard: 'After 60, live dangerously and expect to die.'

While it is a point of view, we do not feel we are living dangerously and do not expect to die cruising. It is probably as safe to cross the

Atlantic these days as to cross a busy street. One reason is that more attention is given to it, more consciousness of possible dangers, more safety equipment carried, and more advice given and heeded. The same scenario for the High Street might go:

'You are going to cross High Street? Have you got your Street Crossing Certificate, North to South? Only South to North, hmm. Have to take someone with you who's got their North to South. Flat shoes only, I'm afraid – those high heels are too dangerous on the crossing. Had a health check, have you – not likely to pass out halfway over and fall under a bus? How's your eyesight and hearing – must be fully aware of the traffic, you know. No, not advisable to push a pram; too distracting, and very dangerous for the occupant. As you know, suitable lights must be carried, and must be shown to be working at all times. The crossing is marked by black and white bands, and an orange beacon flashing isophase. Got your first aid kit? Told the traffic warden you are going to make the attempt? Name and address of your next of kin? Clean knickers on?'

We could remind the young that we too were given our heads when we reached our majority, and that majority continues until we are declared into our second childhood. For the time being, we have gone cruising, staying out all night with those dubious mates of ours, the wind and the sea. We are doing what we want. Don't worry, kids.

Summer sailing, and by this we mean fine weather sailing in season, is really quite simple, and can be undertaken cautiously by people of limited experience who are still capable of learning skills. We feel any-one aged about sixty without much valid experience should consider carefully our chapters in Part Two on medium-term cruising. There we discuss options which would permit increasing or decreasing the commitment in the light of gained experience, and one is not so heavily committed financially to one course of action.

But for those who can sail already, can manage a boat at sea, and who have perhaps long cherished the dream of making a really satis-factory voyage, we would say go ahead. One thing is certain: you will never have another chance, and you might sit for ever in your own backyard watching the grass grow and regretting what might have been. But if you go, do it well. Remember the Royal Naval prayer: 'When thou givest to any of thy servants to endeavour any great matter, it is not the beginning but the continuation of the same until it be thoroughly finished that yieldeth the true glory...' You will probably not be looking for glory, subsfitute contentment.

What is the dream?

To turn one's back on the frenzied noise and acrid air of the cities, and the soggy summer boredom of country towns, and look at a new world of travelling on the water. In the dream, the advantages are

Our sailing barge Hosanna *taken in the little harbour of Angistri.*

obvious: there is peace without boredom, there is useful occupation without taxing an ageing body too heavily, you may choose between continual change of surroundings and people, or you may stay in one area. If you have a cruising boat, your home goes with you, as do whatever little comforts you wish to provide yourself with. Add sunshine and cheap booze, and the mental stimulation so essential to mature minds if one is not to become a vegetable, and we wonder why everyone does not rush for the Mediterranean like lemmings.

Quite a few would say (especially in the queue for the Boat Show) that everyone does, and that those who write glowing and romantic accounts of their cruises contribute to that state of affairs by writing books that appeal to very many dreamers and doers of all ages. Our aim was, and still is, to help people decide whether they want to do it at all, and if so to get it right. We wanted people to avoid ending up with the nightmare side of the dream coin, with He sinking into alcoholism in a quite unsuitable boat in the Med, and She on the plane back to terra firma. Or vice-versa, as has been known.

We went into the knotty subject of personal relations (not to mention elderly ones) in *Sell Up and Sail*. Here we must concentrate on our brief for the ancient mariner. For instance, is long term cruising the right course for them at all?

One of the humbling factors of life at sea is that however much you think you know, and however grand your reputation, one can learn something new from almost everyone one meets. We have no cause to regret anything we have previously written but we are constantly learning more from persons who have come to us for advice; it is a two way process.

The number of people of advanced age going on navigating when all their counsellors and professional busybodies would be advising against it is enormous; we meet them every day. They are doing it because they are happy, or perhaps more realistically, because they are as generally content as all the other factors affecting them allow them to be.

The joys of this life can be summed up by the word independence. One looks after oneself. One can go wherever one is capable of taking the boat, and if in later years that limits one's rovings, well, that's life anyway. It is a healthy life and the lack of interference minimises stress. If and when our political masters eventually introduce compulsory euthanasia for the over-eighties (and Bill does not put it past them), we can move to another country if we are still enjoying life.

Easy cruising
As one grows older one needs a little more comfort. One cannot contort oneself so ably, one's body requires a bit more room, and a bit more ease. For long term living afloat in comfort one really needs a fair-sized boat, and unless you have been intimately used to boats all your life you may find the management of a large boat a bit daunting. There is the maintenance, too. A previous chapter discussed the option of living in a small flat or cottage for the winter and moving afloat for the summer, when living conditions are generally congenial and one can be quite comfortable for the summer season in a smaller boat which is easier to handle.

For those who have always dreamed of the long cruise we will concentrate on a seaworthy boat as a home for a retired couple or a single individual.

We have already said that people are retiring earlier, whether they like it or not. It is not unusual for someone quite senior to be gently eased out of his responsiblities at 50 to 55 to make way for someone of 30 who is full of bright ideas, most of which have already been tried and rejected in his grandfather's day (and probably in his grandfather's before him). Someone, after all has to prevent industry being profitable.

It becomes difficult to find a good job when in one's fifties, and if one has had the good fortune to leave with a reasonable financial settlement, it is worth considering that retirement has already started.

If long-distance cruising attracts you, then now is the time to do what you always wanted to: go cruising for a long period, make that great voyage, never mind the distance, feel the freedom, since now there is nothing to hold you back, and you are no longer restricted to a fortnight, snatched here and there, that must be used whatever the weather. Now you have the time, so get under way before your faculties start to deteriorate.

Start early if you can

You will have more pleasure and benefit from an ocean cruising life if you start while you are still fairly fit, because you will acquire good habits when still adaptable. You can go to places that are not, thank heaven, ameliorated for mass yacht tourism. Being fit, you will still be able to launch dinghies, haul them up beaches, lie alongside fishing boats, see to your own slipping and bottom scrubbing, and moor in bays and anchorages that are not altogether perfect, necessitating a rather more than usual alertness. Not all the time, of course, but you have to be prepared, or at least prepared to be prepared, and you have to avoid getting tired out. (A bit of healthy exhaustion is one thing: flaked right out is quite another.) It is not too late to start at 60 or 65, either.

Age is no barrier

Bill has always taken as his rôle model Admiral Sir Lennon Goldsmith who, on retiring from the Royal Navy, sailed the oceans for many years in a good-sized yacht, and then as he became older and deafer built the lovely little *Diotima*, 32 feet long, probably the first boat ever designed and built specially for navigation by a person very well past his prime. (And probably one of the very best boats, too, in spite of her lack of headroom.) In her the old salt pottered about the Med for another decade, taking a friend as crew when he needed to cover long distances (and he occasionally did), but mostly managing on his own. He died in his 80's of what seemed to have been a heart attack hauling up his anchor in Greece, which is probably just as he wanted. Bill sailed with him several times, and helped look after *Diotima* one bad winter in Malta. The admiral was one of the best.

One of his sayings was that one must pace one's progress. He ensured that everything was within 50% of his capacity, then when it turned out he had made a mistake he would be able to cope. As he aged he made the decision, in his right mind, to abandon the need for extreme caution, as long as no one else was at risk. He was not afraid to die, and lived a full life until he did. As a matter of interest, he carried in his boat full and detailed instructions on what his crew should do if he died at sea. We do not consider this morbid, it never occured to the 24 year old Bill at the time that it was other than common sense in its higher form.

The admiral's views on caution in his 80's are inappropriate to someone of 55. Alertness is necessary. Fitness (and we mean the general overall well-being which can encompass a few aches and imperfections, not the gymnasium hothouse bodybuilding type), is relative. One has to be able to do the things that one sets in train for one's self, and cope with the risks one can reasonably expect. It is always possible to modify expectations and plans to bring events within one's capabilities. Perhaps this is the moment to go into the extra-ordinary large number of disabled persons who cruise long distances or long term.

Deep sea sailing for the disabled

Nothing we say should be taken as demanding total physical fitness as an absolute pre-requisite for cruising. There are many disabled people in boats. Most of them depend to a certain extent on a fit person being available at times. One has to be practical, and one has to consider every case as individual. Some come to mind where the principal sailor is lame or even very lame. One we know says he is less affected by his short leg on board than when ashore. As Laurel knows, you learn to go for'ard up the starboard side, and aft down the port side. (So which leg is the short one?)

It is not generally realised that a person who has lost the use of his legs, for example, can often cope better in a small boat than in a house. The arms become very strong. (The best and quickest over-sixties mast climber we know was very lame from a childhood accident.) Carefully placed hand-holds, and the odd rope hanging from overhead hooks, for example, enable the disabled one to swing about. He has not far to move for anything he needs in his microcosmos. Numberless are such persons who have found they can play a major part in managing and handling a boat. Most leave their wheelchairs in the forepeak for use only when they go ashore. We are aware of various organisations that help with sailing for the disabled, who usually sail in special catamarans where wheelchairs can be used afloat. However, most of the long-term, live-aboard disabled that we have met have lived without wheelchairs in the wheelhouse, in a normal type of boat, with modifications they or their spouse have made themselves.

Going ashore is a problem that has to be solved in a seamanlike manner, like any other. We know one couple who hoist out the disabled one on a derrick, dropping (if that is the right word) her neatly into her wheelchair on the quay; no more difficult than getting the motorbike ashore for younger crews. This lady is an expert navigator. Another, a man who has lost the use of his legs, leads a full social life, hauling himself unselfconsciously along the quaysides with a rather gymnastic use of the hands, though he usually asks for a little assistance crossing gangways. He finds artificial limbs a nuisance unless actually leaving the boat for a period and taking on the profile of a shore-based land crab (his word).

Of course one has to consider the medical aspects of the problem. We do not suppose there is a general solution to any such question. We will discuss this aspect in Chapter 13.

So we conclude that for the newly retired there are few practical limitations on where one can go, nor on what one is capable of doing. In most respects one is a normal cruising person with unlimited time. The best of all worlds; enjoy it to the full.

When we get older
Once one begins to look at lessening general capabilities then the list of cruising grounds gets a little shorter. No more health-giving cruises to look at the penguins in Antarctica, you might think. No more happy little sojourns among the fleshpots of the Kerguelen Islands, followed by carousing in the Cocos, temporising in Tristan da Cuna, and passing the time in Pitcairn. Don't be so sure. There are many very, very old sailors still making these amazing voyages, and we do not mean the Flying Dutchman.

That said, cruising in pleasant areas is easy: what becomes more difficult is the prospect of comfortable passages from one good cruising ground to another. There are plenty of yachtsmen of lesser capabilities swanning about the Caribbean, cruising up and down the American Intracoastal Waterway and taking winters in the Bahamas, or off the coast of Queensland, or in the Med. One can still change areas from time to time, if tiring of one set of scenery, or if politicians foul things up as they seem to do with terrifying frequency. It is just that the long voyage to change cruising grounds needs a little more care and planning and perhaps a little assistance from your friends.

Moving between the Med and the Caribbean has become a little less of a worry for those who are nervous, or whose relatives are nervous, with the arrival of the ARC, or the Atlantic Rally for Cruisers, organised by Jimmy Cornell in collaboration with *Yachting World*. In this, boats travel in a sort of loose convoy, and apart from some idiots who will try to make a race of it, there is no competition to make the less able feel left out. This form of 'organised tour' yachting is contrary to our tastes, but that it has its place and appeals to some is obvious.

Changing boats
It is in this stage of one's cruising career that the choice of boat becomes more critical. How often do you want to change boats? Some

people can do this easily, but once a boat has become personalised in a big way the change is more difficult, both emotionally and practically. The solution that suggests itself for someone starting out fairly late in life is to plan ahead and commence with a suitable boat in which to see out his days.

This is not so easy, given the lack of understanding of the problems by both naval architects and builders, who all tend to think young. (They think it's more fun; they have a pleasant surprise coming one day, have they not?). We have never seen a production boat advertised as ideal for retirement. Usually the marketing people cannot see beyond the bright young things and the Frightful Forties, and are more keen to emphasise bikinis and stowage for the sailboard rather than hot water and walking sticks, while the wheelchairs are only considered under the special heading of Charity with a capital C.

An ex-editor of a yachting magazine had his retirement boat designed for him. We presume some factor changed after he got it, as he soon sold it. We will not comment on its design, except to say that we disagreed with a great many of the features of the boat as described in an article for his magazine.

So if gentlemen as experienced as he and his designer can make such errors, then what chance has the tyro? The humility of ignorance combined with a sharp sense of one's requirements can sometimes be an advantage.

We will tackle the problem of boat design later.

We have mentioned the desirability of choosing a boat to last a long time, or in the passive mood, not changing boats very often. There is, however, a case for a person who is still quite fit on comparatively early retirement envisaging or allowing for one change of boat in the future. Someone who retires in the late 50s or very early 60s might well have the prospect of over 20 years of cruising ahead of them, and cruising for the 80-year-old has to be rather different from that for the 60-year-old. Perhaps with increasing age one can consider slipping into the mode of part-time cruising that we discussed in Chapter 6. There would be several indicators that such a change is due: the need to consult doctors with increasing frequency and the more frequent need for a helping hand, a pause while your mind catches up with your will, and your body catches up with both of them, the need for a time to get your thoughts in order. But if you do change mode, do not lay yourself up completely in your off season. Have a refit, some new paintwork, do some research into the places you have visited already (there is always more to know about places hastily visited). We have been interested to notice that after a winter when we continued cruising (more gently, it is true), we were in far better shape this spring than we normally are after lazy winter months not doing very much.

On the other hand, in the following autumn, after 18 months of being continually on the go, we began to detect signs of fatigue and a need to slow down.

Motor or sail?

There are so many open questions about long-term cruising that we cannot go deeply into the matter here. What we can do is to consider any special features desirable in boats dedicated to this type of cruising with mature owners in the first flush of wisdom.

Here it is possible to advance the notion that in some ways ocean sailing is easier for the less agile than pottering about the Med. In the Med one makes shortish hops in less than ideal sailing weather, with possibly awkward berthing and unberthing at each end. The old saying that in the Med there is either too much wind or too little is not wrong. What compounds the problem is the frequency of change between the two conditions. Add this to a tendency for the wind direction to shift every couple of hours and one spends one's time pulling sails up and down like national flags at the end of the British Empire. It can be quite exhausting. After an afternoon of that, and a late summer thunderstorm, one has a temptation to turn into a motor cruiser and power into the port, easier still an anchorage. What's wrong with that?

Why not be a motor cruiser? Why go through all this ritual of hanging ineffective flappy bits about the boat? One answer is that we like to think we give ourselves something to do all day. Another is that crossing oceans needs a lot of fuel. Another is the feeling that it is not quite nice to be a motor cruiser, and a yacht looks prettier. Many people just love sailing.

Josephine on *Blue Mallard*, an out-and-out sailing yacht, put it this way. 'We watched a yacht come in to an anchorage recently; they pushed a button and the sails furled, another button and the anchor went out, then they poured some drinks and I was surprised they hadn't a button for that too. To me that isn't sailing.' We asked if any other device would make life easier for her, and she admitted that they were hoping to put in an electric anchor windlass.

For a person past his prime motor cruising is a good option. It would be better done in a motor-sailer in the size of boat most of us are thinking about. Not because the sails are necessary for progress, but they do help reduce the motion in a lumpy sea, and give you some kind of power of movement if the engine breaks down. (We have observed how people polarise into those who do not feel safe without an engine to back up the sails, and those who do not feel safe without sails to back up the engine.)

In our opinion, this Dutch-built boat is a good steady motor cruiser for longer term cruising. The photo was taken in Aegina.

It would be best, in our opinion, to have a boat of moderate speed, one that does not plane. The fast boats eat fuel; we have just come across one who would spend £1500 if he motored for a full 12-hour day, though in that time he could cover some 250 miles, at a price of £6 per mile. Only the well-heeled could do a lot of cruising at that rate.

Even in a moderate-sized, moderately engined boat the fuel costs are not negligible. Most fourstroke diesels in a boat of between 30 and 40 feet consume 0.25 litres of diesel oil per horsepower per hour at cruising speeds. So an engine developing 30 hp when driving the boat at 6 knots would use about 1.25 litres per mile.

This usually makes people think a bit about adding some sails, especially if you fear, as we do, that the cost of fuel oil is more likely to rise than fall. In the Med even a sailing boat is likely to do about 500 hours of engine work a year if she spends a good deal of the time passage-making, and if needing the engine for refrigeration, etc.

Not only does the Med involve one in a lot of agile sail shifting, but one enters harbour rather more frequently than the ocean sailor.

Perhaps this is the essence of cruising anyway, the places rather than the voyage, but it is certainly the case in the Med. The harbours tend to be more crowded and the berths perhaps a bit less convenient than when the odd yacht could tuck itself in some out of the way corner. It is our experience, watching our brethren in many different ports, that berthing in crowded harbours causes yachtsmen more *sturm und drang* than any other part of cruising. It is so much easier to be able to toss out the anchor at the end of the day in an uncluttered bay.

By contrast the cross-Atlantic sailor is more inclined to suffer boredom than broken arms. He actually has to make a special effort to tweak his sheets every couple of days to avoid the possibility of chafe. He is more likely to go round looking for something to do. Laurel made herself a three-string dulcimer on one of our crossings, having time to spare after catering, baking bread, watch-keeping and mending the sails. Bill thought she could have done something useful, but she felt that that was not the point.

Nevertheless, it is a fact that more older folk end up pottering about the Med or the Intracoastal Waterway than crossing oceans. This is very possibly because they calculate, even if instinctively, that if they have, say, only 4000 days of life expectancy, then spending 30 at a time doing exactly the same thing and with exactly the same view is not using that time to the best advantage. In the end:

> Med versus Ocean,
> and motor v sail
> is down to emotion
> and who wags the tail ...

And preference of course. There is a wide divergence of preferences, and that is a very good thing.

Inside the boat

We still believe that the production boat, while it has its uses for short distances and fortnightly holidays, is not the best answer for long term living-in. The chief problem in a production boat is one of stowage, and for less agile people the stowage has to be more readily accessible. It seems as if most designers provide the stowage in those bits of boat that are left over after fitting the 'features', whereas we think a live-aboard boat should have its stowages considered as an important feature *per se*.

Banned should be the bottomless locker that you can only reach into with a long boat-hook. In fact there is an argument for replacing lockers with drawers, an expensive alternative, but very helpful for those of us who may have the first twinges of arthritis.

We would like to give the boatyard Moody's their due. The Moody Owners' Club (a lovely-sounding body like the Loose Women's Institute, or the Ugley Girls' School Choir) made representations to the company about how things could be improved, especially from the female point of view: details in the design of bunks, galley and heads for example. The Moody builders listened to the Moody owners and improved their product. This is excellent news; builders of production boats *should* listen to such feedback, and judging by some of the continental boats we have seen this year, there is a need for the *oreille ouverte* on the other side of the Channel too.

The essential features for a mature mariner in the accommodation of a live-aboard yacht are:

- Ease of moving about with good headroom.
- A level cabin sole, or floor, without any of those irritating little three inch steps.
- Plenty of good handholds and rounded corners.
- A bunk or bunks that can be made without having a wrestling match and losing the skin off the knuckles.
- The heads (WC) pump (and the WC itself) must be accessible for use, cleaning, and dismantling without major contortions; all seacocks must be easily accessible.
- The engine and any generator or fridge machinery must be accessible to any routine maintenance points without having to dismantle half the boat's furnishings.
- The galley should give the cook a chance to sit if she, or he, prefers to cook sitting down (much the same applies to the chart table). It should not be necessary to reach across a lighted stove to get at things which are frequently needed.
- The switchboard should have switches of a reasonable size for arthritic fingers, and labels that can be read without glasses.

Not essential, but adds to the comfort:
- A second head, a good idea if the boat is big enough. A failed or blocked head is quite a disaster, and requires urgent attention usually at inconvenient times. When one is tired, the chance to leave it until tomorrow is very valuable. And heads *do* get blocked without it being anyone's fault.
- In the saloon it is nice to have the dining arrangements separate from the comfortable seating. One can sit upright at the table, which is the best way, and then on the opposite side of the boat perhaps, a deep settee, or even two built-in easy chairs for those quiet evenings when the weather does not allow sitting on deck. We saw this arrangement excellently carried out in the Cape Town-

built yacht, *Duet* (a Petersen design, we think); it was ordered specially for the retired couple who live aboard her, and is one of the most sensibly fitted yachts for such cruising we have ever seen.

- If you have guest accommodation it is pleasant to have it well separated from one's own.

- How very welcome is a hot bath when arthritis appears, (sea-water can be used, heated in a couple of black shower bags such as everyone in sunny climes carries these days) followed by a rinsing shower. Not all of us have arthritis at 60, but it affects a very large number by the age of 70. And even the non-arthritic get a few aching bones and muscles from time to time. Why suffer? There is no need of a big, full-size bath; some quite small ones are available on the continent, smaller than we have found in the catalogues in Britain or USA. One was four feet long, only a bare two feet wide and about fifteen inches deep; that is not very big, and could form the basis of a shower tray anyway, but it is big enough to get the hips immersed. It could go under the floorboards over the keel in boats that have a V-section, or in glassfibre boats it could even be moulded into the keel. In fact strange shaped baths can now be so easily made that you could almost fit one under the side decks. Well, why not? Quite apart from its cleansing and therapeutic purposes the bath is a good place to fling wet clothes or oilies if you have not the time to deal with them at sea. One does not usually bath at sea; it can make you seasick.

That about covers aspects that are peculiar to the long term live-aboard. There are other aspects of boat design and fittings that are relevant to older persons, but because they apply also to boats other than for long term cruising, we will look at them in the next chapter.

10

A Boat to Grow Old In

> I saw three ships go sailing by
> One was built like Noah's first try
> One would never have kept me dry
> But one was the apple of a mariner's eye

IN EACH CHAPTER where it was appropriate we have written something about boats and their design, and in this and chapter 11 we
are going to gather together some of the common features, reviewing
those more important from the point of view of the less agile, and discuss boats in general.

Strictly speaking, anyone retiring at or about the normal age does
not need to consider any special features in his boat. A person of pensionable age has all the faculties he needs to cope with the same boat
as his junior of 20 years. But he cannot look forward to keeping those
faculties intact for 20 more years; those he has will attenuate at an
ever-accelerating rate.

Thus someone aged 55 or 60 may feel that he is fine for the next
few years. However, if he contemplates change this chapter may help,
especially if he wishes to cut down the number of future changes.
Changing boats is usually agonising. One grieves for the old love, and
has doubts about the new.

Change or adaptation?

We changed our boat/home at the age of 60, and it was an experience
that took three years, and was at the same time exhilarating and miserable. There was an element of 'The King is dead, long live the King'
about it; an odd mixture of mourning and self-indulgence, leaving
one's moral sense as confused as if one's mother had died at the same
time as a child was being born, and one did not know what sort of
party to give. It took a lot out of us, but was necessary as our beloved

Fare Well, a ketch of about 34 tons, was becoming rather more than the two of us could handle. Nothing had yet gone wrong, but the writing was on the bulkhead.

If you have the sort of boat that is kept in a marina to be used for a few week-ends and perhaps for a fortnight's holiday once a year, then changing a boat can be as easy as changing a car. Drive to the dealer's, toss him the keys, transfer the dinglum-danglums if they happen to mean something to you, and drive away the new one. But changing a boat you spend half your time in, or live in, is altogether a different experience. One becomes attached to a boat in a way that applies to no other artefact. This is very possibly because the boat may well have saved your life by performing in a manner you had no right to expect from an apparently inanimate object. It might also have come close to killing you on occasions, but that sentiment occasionally appears even in the best of partnerships.

When and if the boat is anthropomorphised into a person then you have a real problem changing. Better to find the right boat for long-term ownership and develop a good relationship with it. It is likely, one must also remember, that as you get older you will become less adaptable, and the boat you have become accustomed to over the years will tax your faculties less than a new one which could give you some nasty surprises. You might consider adapting the one you have rather than going for something new and probably strange.

All this does not apply so much to boats that you will own for occasional pottering or short-term cruising, which will represent a much less important slice of your life. Even here, though, you have to expect that your aptitude for do-it-yourself will decrease with time and all those little things like cradles, props, stowages for the mast in winter and so on that you have made over several years will have suddenly become rather more difficult to replace from your own resources.

So let us consider a boat that will stand a chance of providing you with some long-term satisfaction. Because we have discussed so many differing aspects of sailing, so we will have to diversify the discussion into all sorts of creeks and crannies of the nautical scene, and some of these we have already explored a little under specific sections. Nevertheless we would urge readers who are with us thus far to read this chapter, because no person, and certainly no boat, is ever capable of being plonked firmly into one pigeon-hole: there are always compromises and overlaps.

A boat for long-term ownership

There are a few basic principles that govern selection of a boat in any circumstances, and though some of these might be considered obvious, we will go through them to clarify our thoughts as well as yours.

The boat should be seaworthy for the type of use and the area in which she will be used. Seaworthy in this context includes suitability for waters other than the open sea, if appropriate. That is self-evident, but the boat should be examined critically, for boats are often less suitable for one use than another. Local factors, such as shoal waters, types of mooring available and ease of access to them, the availability of shelter in the event of a change of weather, are all variables in this equation.

The prime cost of the craft must take into account a margin to allow for the essential personalisation that can turn an artefact into a treasured possession, and for those repairs and alterations whose necessity did not show up at the time of purchase, but certainly will afterwards.

The boat must be *very easily* handled by the crew you envisage having, so that a smaller crew could cope in an emergency. This is not merely a question of sail-changing and steering; it has also to do with berthing, for we have noticed that more people get into difficulties when berthing than they do at sea. One must also consider dealing with the boat when she is out of her element on shore. This is all lumbago and bad back territory. The size of boat you choose should fit both your capability and your pocket.

The boat and her gear must be simple to service or repair. Essential spare parts should be easily available, and repair facilities must be adequate in the waters where you intend to use her. This latter may be hard to assess if you are contemplating moving your area of operation. But the assessment has to be made. If a boat can be said to conform to those general principles we are on the way to a suitable choice. One then needs to look at the special requirements for the classifications we have looked at. These, as we have said, will overlap.

Racing or pottering?

For one-design or class racing the choice of boat narrows to:

- Those classes which are raced in the area that interests you.
- Those which are within your means, both physical and financial.
- Those for which you can find a convenient mooring in the area that interests you.

This would rule out those classes that require such a degree of athleticism as to verge on the outrageous. There are, however, some local classes that provide good racing without straining the sinews more than is good for you. Our rule of thumb is that if it requires special physical training then it stops being a pleasure and becomes a *sport*, and there is a disturbing tendency for sports these days to be taken too seriously.

Whether for racing or pottering about in a day-boat, a keel boat that can be kept on moorings has the advantage that launching and hauling-out are thus minimised, it being these activities that often need more energy and pose more risk of injury than the actual sailing.

Trailer sailers

On the other hand it can be a good idea to have a boat which can be trailed home for the winter season: the trailer makes a serviceable cradle for storage, and the saving in storage costs is considerable. There is also the convenience of the boat near your back door for the next season's tart-up, and the availability of power points for electric tools, so that you may enjoy some do-it-yourself modifications. Launching or hauling out a small keel boat is best done by crane, which makes the transfer to or from a trailer much easier; it is therefore obvious that you would need access to a crane.

Slipways for launching non-keel trailer sailers are to be found in many places, and this opens up the prospect of sailing other than in your home area.

Keel boats

The main reason for a keel boat is that it presents a more stable platform. One's reactions will get slower in time, and in the unballasted centreboarder the ability to react swiftly to changing forces is one of the principal facets of the sailing technique. This morning we saw a very old man trying to land a heavy object from a small plastic tender bobbing like a cork in a millrace. He was quite unable to do so unaided (indeed he fell heavily) because he could not cope rapidly enough with the disturbance to the centre of gravity of the whole ensemble when he moved the load.

Cruising boats

It is when one comes to cruising boats that the problems of choice start to present themselves in formidable array, because we not only have to consider the berthing and sailing, but also the question of accommodation, even if only for the long-weekender. Again there are some basic principles, which will apply to all except perhaps the specialised canal boat, which is another matter.

For local cruising, which will be mainly in the smaller types of boat, one is constrained by the market, for it is usually necessary to buy a production boat of some sort, and there are none to our knowledge specially designed and built for the mature sailor. That does not rule them out *per se*, for though it is unlikely that any production boat would meet our criteria 100%, we have to admit that even boats which we have designed ourselves would not do that. Everything is a compromise, and there are no absolutes in practice.

Boats that suggest a nautical disaster ...

The overall impression – what to look for
Boats that suggest a nautical disaster (and we have seen several that
we think fit such a description) should be dismissed from your mind at
once. Unfortunately the libel laws inhibit us from listing them, but you
will recognise them by an atmosphere of awkwardness, of too much
crammed in to too little, of boxiness, ugliness, too much height for too
little length or the reverse. Their curves are jerky and unrelated, there
is no sweetness in the lines, and there is no health in them. They have
an air of being a nautical caravan. The marine necessities take second
place to the fripperie. Often they have brand names suggesting the
deep ocean for which they would be manifestly unsuitable, or their
foreign manufacturers have named the class with an emotive English
word that is so inapt as to be inept, meaningless. Generally such boats
are sold rather than bought. There is a distinction. There may be a lot
of them about because good salesmen can always take advantage of
inexperienced people, but these boats are not sought after by people
who know boats.

The pretty boat
You may think that we are being over-sentimental in advising people
to buy a pretty boat. We do not think so. What are termed nice lines

are a convention that has come about over the years, not from scientific theory but via the observation of seamen whose lives have depended on the things they notice. These shapes have come to be associated with safety and comfort, and even with survival, and it is this that makes us consider them pretty.

The present-day convention for sailing yachts that look like grandma's flat-iron upside down (and the yachts are rather too often to be found in that condition) is due not to some recently discovered enhancement of seaworthiness, but to the influence of a lunatic racing rating rule, which laid less emphasis on beam measurements than on depth. This contrasts with an older racing rating rule which did the reverse and led to a fashion of narrow-gutted, very deep-draughted yachts (the so-called plank-on-edge type) which were likewise not very seaworthy. The lesson is that racing designers never get it right for cruisers. Well, hardly ever.

Moderation in all things; no boat should be extreme, and we would go so far as to say that any pretty boat is likely to be a good boat with few vices. Try her first, though; she may bite.

Unsteady boats: the initial righting moment

> Seesaw, my tea's on the floor,
> Captain says pick it up faster,
> Despite all my talents I'm losing my balance;
> This vessel should have a new master.

A righting moment is the force that restores a boat to the upright condition when something displaces her from it. It is the force, therefore, that stops a boat heeling over too much, too quickly, as you move about.

One of the first things to look for is a boat which begins to come upright as soon as she starts to heel. A stiff boat, in other words. A righting force that comes into play at the first shift from the upright is not a result of a deep keel with a lot of lead on it. Contrary to popular opinion, the weight of the keel only helps the righting when the boat has already reached a fair angle of heel and the keel is effectively at the side rather than underneath. You used to get a good demonstration of this in older boats with heavy, galvanised-iron centreboards. The *initial* stability did not change much whether the centre-board was up or down.

A good initial righting moment is a function of hull shape, and the total weight of the boat; the fixed keel helps initial stability by increasing the total weight. The diagrams in Appendix 1 may help understand the concept.

Multihulls

There is one type of boat that merits our special consideration, and that is the multihull. We have talked about initial stability, and this is one of the most dramatic features of the multihull. It is bought at the expense of a loss of righting moment at large angles of heel (hence all those deep-sea racing catamarans that capsize), but in the cruising type, sensibly handled, this is seldom a serious factor, and there are devices available to make the event even less likely.

It is this initial stability that gives the multihull an advantage. One has the opportunity to move about a platform that is far less likely to tip, especially in harbour, and thus the potential for accidents is much reduced. Another advantage is that one gets more accommodation for the size and cost of the boat, and for our purposes this means a larger area of level floor.

There are some compensating disadvantages. The accommodation as a whole is often arranged a little oddly, especially in the smaller ones, because full headroom is only available in the two hulls, and thus the saloon joining the hulls has limited headroom over part or all, though the Oceanic catamaran has pretty good headroom throughout on a length of 30 feet.

We have come across several accidents caused by people falling down the steep ladders necessary to pass from the higher cross-deck to the bottom of the floats. Watch this weak point in multihull designs. One has to go up to quite a size to get good headroom throughout on one level. This could mean that you would be contemplating driving a mobile tennis court.

The other noticeable disadvantage is the lack of welcome given to these boats by some harbour authorities. They do take up more berthing area than a monohull, and they are often asked to pay extra, which is probably fair; the question is: how much extra? Some modern yachts have such extreme beam that they are very little narrower than a catamaran, yet we have known marinas demand double fees from a cat. That really is too much; perhaps 25 to 50% extra is reasonable, and is the most common surcharge.

Catamarans do not carry the load that a monohull can without losing some of their seaworthiness, but the room to move about easily cannot be lightly dismissed. For every plus there is a minus.

It is sometimes difficult to get an unbiased opinion on multihulls from experienced sailors because they tend to polarise in their preferences in this respect. We are monohull people, but we have tried very hard to be objective because this is an important topic, and one has to base an opinion on rather a narrower viewpoint in the context of this book. Whatever one's personal view, there is one fact that cannot be gainsaid: a large number of elderly cruising people who have had, or who still sail a catamaran, would not contemplate any other type for their old age. We cannot think of one old person who, having sailed catamarans, would not agree with that, and we have discussed this subject widely.

Many of the good cruising catamarans come from British builders who are acknowledged to be above average for workmanship. Second-hand examples are often available, but the market is not so active as for monohulls. It may be necessary to wait to be able to buy a good example, and similarly one may have to wait for a buyer if selling.

Catamarans have their place in the canals also, provided their over-all beam is less than the lock width. Their width is, in fact, an asset on Continental canals, for we have said in considering boats for canals that it is more comfortable in locks if the boat is nearly as broad as the lock is wide. In French locks, for example, this is 5 metres, and you need a lot of monohull to carry that beam.

Sails

On deck the important thing is to have everything arranged for handling without acrobatics. We like the idea of all sails on rollers, and in the sizes of boat we are talking about there is no need of power rollers. All the sheets and furling lines should come to the cockpit. A storm jib on its own roller well inside the stem is worth considering for offshore cruising. So is a well-divided rig (several small sails instead of two large ones) that cuts down the likelihood of reefing; we have found it better to take in a sail completely rather than shorten all of several. Our reason is that part rolling sails in strong winds almost always leads to some distortion in the canvas, and puts unfair loads on certain parts of the sail; all right for a stop-gap measure but not desirable as a policy. If the rig is well-conceived one should be able to juggle the sail plan without unsettling the balance. Of course in smaller boats the sloop rig is necessary or one would end up setting a multitude of pocket handkerchiefs, but bear in mind that the acts of reefing and unreefing in the open sea are peculiarly prone to mishaps and accidents. Reefing at sea is often done when you are drymouthed, anxious, and in already roughening seas, while shaking out the reef can happen when you are tired and beginning to relax your vigilance because danger is passing.

It is best not to have too large a genoa with the sloop rig. Repeatedly tacking a jib with a large overlap is very tiring, and though one can always reef in a bit of the jib, this is not such a good idea in stronger winds. This is less important with longer distance cruising boats which tend to enter or leave moorings under power, but with smaller, and dayboats, which might manoeuvre right up to moorings, it is a factor.

With an all-rolling sail plan the canvas can be slightly overweight, thus reducing problems due to failure of stitching or cloth; with sails more or less permanently bent on, the weakening due to the ultra-violet in sunlight is more rapid than when sails are stowed away under covers.

We are not convinced of the value of sacrificial strips. We once had two sails of identical cloth set, one with and one without strip, and both had the same life.

Heaving-to

We are firmly of the opinion that a boat should be able to heave-to safely, if there is plenty of searoom. That is to lie with a few small sails set so that she keeps the same aspect to the wind, while making very little way through the water. This is the best and safest way a crew can recover if they get over tired. It is a very good way of surviving really bad weather, and harbouring your resources. The trouble is that not all boats will do so docilely. Yachting magazine reviews of boats ought to give some guidance on this but because their trials are subject to the lottery of the weather on a particular day, it is something that gets overlooked. If you are buying a boat, try to have a trial on a choppy day, and get the seller to demonstrate heaving-to for you. If the crew cannot have a little siesta without twitching the rig every five minutes the boat may not be for you.

As a generalisation we think that short keel boats do not heave to so well as longer keel boats, but there are numerous exceptions: the facility must be considered as idiosyncratic to the boat.

Gaffers

When this book was first under discussion the editor said, 'Not too much about old gaffers'; or words to that effect. We do not know which of us gives the impression that old gaffers are our obsession. While we love a pretty boat of any age, in fact neither of us is deeply committed to any particular rig for all purposes. Undoubtedly the Bermudan rig is paramount for serious racing, while the lugsail is ideal for simple pottering in a small boat. For cruising in the context of this book the prime requirement is simplicity, and saving effort. Sad to say, however picturesque, a gaff rig is not the best under either of those headings.

The reasons are in its weight aloft; you have to hoist a heavy spar as well as the sail, and if lowering in difficult conditions you have to tame the spar and get it under control before it injures you. Another important contra-indication in our view is the fact that the gaff sail does not lend itself to modern roller reefing.

Junks

Some people swear by the junk rig, which allows the sail to be controlled using what are in effect full length battens, which have recently come into fashion; amazing, isn't it? what the bright boys can discover by examining the practices of the ancients. We had a look at the original junk rig while we were in China, and even when simplified by Blondie Haslar, we think it has rather too much string. One would want to get used to it early in life to be able to manage it well in old age. The principle of fully-battened sails, on the other hand, is one we wholeheartedly endorse.

Lateen

For smaller boats we have seen an interesting rig, which is experimental and might interest eccentric professors. (They retire too, do they not?). This is a development of the lateen rig that was so effective for centuries in the Mediterranean. The long canted spar has two rolled up lateen sails, one either side of the mast. For beating to windward the lee sail is used, while for running before the wind both sails are unfurled. There is only one sheet and rolling line for each sail, and the spar is left aloft. Tacking is remarkably simple: furl one sail and set the other; it can be done in seconds and is less trouble than hauling a genoa round the mast.

Bermudan rig

We said we like having all the sails on rollers. With the Bermudan rig the main can roll into the mast, or downwards into the boom. The latter we have seen working very well, and it appeals to us. The gear can mostly be reached from deck level; anything that goes wrong can be seen to without climbing the mast, and one also avoids the howling, wailing organ-pipe effect of the vertical slot in the after side of the mast when in a strong wind. Makers of these in-mast gears say they have solved this problem; perhaps they have in their test-rigs, but we who have to lie next to these vessels on blustery nights know they have not. The crew of a new boat we moored next to this year in Limnos in a strong *meltemi* wind wore earplugs, and had the courtesy to offer us some. This is too high a price to pay for 'progress'.

Unless you have a strong wish to play with the rig of your boat (and why not if you are capable of doing so? You could start a new career as a researcher into the aerodynamics of sails), it is better to have a tried and tested one and we are, we think, back to the Bermudan sloop with the sails on rollers for the smaller sizes of boat, with perhaps the ketch cutter for the larger. It might be better for the less active to have several small sails to control and handle than two large ones. If things go wrong, and one day they will, the sheer effort in taming a big sail that is apparently intent on tearing itself apart and/or beating your brains out in a strong wind, especially when you are short-handed, is immense, and the forces involved can be lethal.

To set against this is the amount of time to be taken to set, trim or furl a number of sails, so that one often sets fewer than one should. 'What! Get all that lot up for only half an hour?' Mmm. But at least you have the option.

Rigging and masting

It is essential that standing rigging and masting be *massively over-strength*, even if not planning to go deeply into the sunset. An older person has not got the physical reserves to cope with more serious disasters such as mast loss. We know of two occasions where an elderly sailor has got into serious trouble this way. It makes sense for younger cruisers too; cruising yachtsmen do not want the very last ounce of performance out of their yachts; of far more importance is security and reliability. The possibility and likelihood of stainless steel failure due to metal fatigue or stress corrosion increases exponentially as the actual load approaches the break-strain. If the normal working stress can be kept to a small proportion of the break-strain, it is likely that stress corrosion or metal fatigue will never manifest itself at all, even over very long periods indeed. In this way the extra cost of the strong fittings and wires will more than repay themselves in the long run, both in the extra sense of security and financially, too. Our ketch *Fare Well* came through Hurricane Alberto north of Bermuda with no damage to masts or rigging in spite of a knock-down.

Shelter

One feature that receives too little attention in most cruising boats is shelter for the helmsman and crew. At our age this is already important, and as years advance it becomes even more so. Shelter is needed from both the sun and from the various forms and types of water that can be thrown at us, but also shelter from the cold. We, ourselves, usually sail in warmer waters and in comparatively calm conditions and prefer to go downwind, when it is pleasant to handle the vessel on deck in the open. (We haven't always subscribed to the philosophy that Gentlemen Do Not Tack, but have adapted to it in recent years.) It is at these times that a good awning is desirable. You will get a healthy tan soon enough; in fact you may have trouble avoiding looking like a wrinkled brown walnut if you are not careful to stay under your awning as much as possible.

For a smallish boat with an average-sized cockpit the American Bimini awning is very effective. It can be used while actively sailing as well as in harbour and it folds away neatly when not in use, for at the

The Bimini awning. It is very easy to put up or take down, and can be spread when sailing.

beginning and end of the season you may not wish it to be spread. In harbour in very hot weather it might need supplementing with a light-weight larger awning offering more comprehensive cover, perhaps with side half-curtains. One hears a lot about the elderly being suscep-tible to hypothermia, and it is this end of the temperature variation that is emphasised in cold Britain. But hyperthermia, that is the dangerously raised temperature associated with heat exhaustion and heat-stroke are just as dangerous, and older folk are not so able to detect the first signs of these dangerous conditions.

In our view, the canvas dodger does not offer adequate shelter against the elements. Nor does the simple dog-house, given that more than one dog might need to be sheltered under it. There is no reason why a boat over 35 feet, say, cannot have a small wheelhouse as well as a good on-deck steering and conning position. To anyone who has nearly drowned in a tropical rain squall the idea must appeal. The rain falls so as to give one the feeling of total immersion, the drops bounce up and under simple shelters, and though the water is warmish, to get one's breath can be physically exhausting. So what if your view is lim-ited? you cannot see anything in a rainstorm like that, anyway; even seeing the stemhead is unlikely.

Then there is the question of sailing when the weather is not so reliable or warm, as at the beginning or end of the season when weather is capricious and often suddenly cold and inhospitable. Oh, how lovely is a wheelhouse in those conditions! Tucked in warm with a cup of cocoa in the night watches. Yes, the sheets and guys are cleated outside, but they can all be within easy reach. We suggest that this sort of comfort becomes important as the years advance. One feels the cold more, and bones ache. Never mind the macho, feel the comfort. In really advanced age the body is slow to respond to dangerous changes of temperature, and anything that will help to insulate the person is worth looking into. Hypothermia is no longer a theoretical problem.

Fresh water

Surely this must be the same problem for all ages? No, it is not. It is important in the boats we are contemplating that there is adequate water tankage to last longer than a young crew would need. Watering ship by jerrican is just not on any more. A five-gallon jerrican of fresh water weighs 50 lbs, which is far too much to carry, and even that is not very much volume of water from a domestic point of view, meaning that several journeys, perhaps of some length, must be made. Remember that not all ports have conveniently placed fresh water taps.

One *must* be able to water ship by hose, and have the tankage to ensure that one does not run short in ports where there is no tap close enough for a hose run, or where there is no supply at all. Carry 25 metres minimum of hose, and a collection of threaded adaptors.

Obviously the total tankage required is dependent on the variables: size of boat, size of crew, length and locality of the envisaged cruise, and the certainty of your knowledge of the facilities in the ports to be visited. If you are cruising warm climes, then you will find extra water a very welcome luxury. Do not stint yourselves.

11

Boats and Gear

Humpty Dumpty went up the mast
Humpty D came down rather fast
All the King's horses were no use at all
They couldn't embark as the boat was too small

Mishaps and the design of cruising boats

If we consider how, when, and where the majority of mishaps occur to sailors who have impaired mobility for whatever reason, we can decide how these might affect the design of their boats.

- The first risk is while berthing.
- The second is when boarding or leaving the boat.
- The third is while cooking.
- The fourth is while going aloft or attending to rigging. (This is very possibly the most potentially dangerous activity, but you do not have to do it very often, if at all).
- The fifth is at sea in moderately rough weather, both on deck, but more often below (more in moderately rough weather than in very rough seas, because in a storm one is not only tuned to take special care, but also because in very serious weather one does less because there is less that one can do).

The lesson is to give a lot of attention to the small things that cause or mitigate these mishaps. The problems attaching to seagoing accidents tend to affect us all irrespective of age, but the young may wish to exchange extra security against performance. That would be unwise at an age that should bring wisdom.

General risks are reduced by good hand-holds and lifelines on deck, by non-slip surfaces, and high, strong guard rails (not at all common, but by no means impossible to add to most boats as an after-job).

Berthing

Gone are the days when one could sail into any harbour and manhandle the boat into an alongside berth. Now, especially in the Med, the

110

harbours are often crowded, and one needs to be a bit thrusting and determined to get a good berth. Recently in Limnos, two yachts arriving late in the evening anchored off for the night, to await the first departures of the morning, which was sensible and good mannered. In some ports, notably those near big cities where ill-mannered motorboaters congregate, the weekends can become nightmares of pushing, shoving, jostling craft, piling up higgledy-piggledy several deep against the boats already moored end-on, at all hours of the day or night. It is something so horrible that you have to experience it at least once to understand the nadir of yachting. It is also unseamanlike. (This is not a diatribe against all motor yachtsmen; only against a certain type.)

Mediterranean mooring
We offer some thoughts on Med mooring, and how it might be achieved with minimum effort, as it affects the design and gear of your boat. The problem is that some boats lend themselves poorly to boarding over the ends, a facility that cruising-boat designers of most nationalities seem never to take into account. There are two options: anchor and bows-to, or anchor and stern-to.

Anchors and cables
Whichever way round you moor in fine weather, a single good anchor in firm holding ground is going to do all the work that is necessary to hold your boat in position. As the anchor and cable will extend out at right-angles to the shore, all boats moored end-on to the same quay avoid the awful problems of untangling foul anchors and crossed cables. Or should do in the best of possible worlds, Captain Murphy serves at sea, too. And everyone is baffled when mooring at the angle of two quays.

It is in suspect weather, when strong winds are blowing or are in the offing, that one has to be prudent and skilful with anchors. Our solution in *Hosanna* where load carrying is not important, is to have a stern anchor and cable of twice the expected size for a vessel of her tonnage, relying on the extra holding power to take the magnified strain a cross wind puts on an anchor in these circumstances. In this way we are able to avoid most of the problems of anchor cables getting crossed, at least by us.

This is not necessarily the best solution from the point of view of the ship's security. The most effective remedy for a changeable strong wind in these conditions is to lay out two anchors on long cables, so that the angle between the cables when they leave your ship is about twenty degrees (This applies whether bows- or stern-to.) Evidently, this is bound to lead to crossed cables if everybody does it, and it is only widely practised when laying up for a period. Nevertheless, it is a good practice when conditions demand it, and it does enable one to relax and get a bit of peace without that nagging anxiety that can murder sleep more effectively than Macbeth.

Given that all persons of our age having boats that can be lived in even for comparatively short periods, should equip them with self-stowing anchors and cables, the inference is that one end at least should have double equipment. The problem is weight.

At the bows one needs one bower anchor with about 75 metres of chain cable for anchoring anywhere in whatever conditions. In harbours one generally does not need that length out, though it is worth remembering that cable in the locker is not making much contribution to the safety of the ship; it is cable on the sea bed that counts.

The second bower anchor could have, say, 45 metres of chain and be completely self-stowing. All that is a lot of weight, and you begin to understand why a proper cruising boat should be a load carrier. It is also quite a problem for the designer to allow for this weight which has to be well forward. But the oft-given advice not to put weight in the ends of the boat is not always the best. Weight at bow and stern can reduce the pitching moment, and make the boat a little more steady in a rough sea, at the expense of having more spray over the deck. We prefer, on balance, to have the weight in the ends, accepting the concomitant slight loss of performance to windward with equanimity.

It would be possible, of course, to lighten the weight by having only 12 metres of chain on the second bower and back it up with 100 metres of braided nylon. One could still bring the chain tail to its own cable-holder to weigh and stow the anchor by power, the rope being comparatively easy to bring in when there is no weight on it. Keep the rope coiled in a small dust bin, from which it will run out easily when needed, and have little opportunity to tie itself into a spaghetti knot.

How does the above translate itself to stern anchors? Quite well. It is possible to have a normally rigged single bower with its 75 metres of chain for conventional anchoring, and a stern anchor and chain cable with its own cable-holder and drum aft. One would not need so much chain cable aft, only about 50 metres.

The second stern anchor with about 12 metres of chain, and its 100 metres of nylon, would have to be a mobile one, to be used aft if needed, and to make a stand-by bower if needed there. No normal boat could reasonably carry an anchor with a full measure of chain cable at each of its four corners, but some good old heavy boats could. Whatever the solution, money spent on mechanical assistance for lifting and stowing heavy loads like anchors and cables is not wasted; from our not inconsiderable experience in most of the world's waters we think a power windlass, for anchors over 25 lbs, will repay you over and over again.

The bows-to option

One of the simplest ways of berthing a small or medium sized boat end-on is to use a stern anchor and put the bows to the quay. This makes a lot of sense, for very often the water is shallower close to the quay, and a deep-hung rudder is vulnerable to damage. It is also easier to manoeuvre the boat into a narrow slot when going ahead than when reversing.

For smaller boats a composite cable of a short length of chain with a longer one of nylon is best. This short chain/nylon anchor cable is comparatively easy to handle, and flotilla companies have devised very simple ways in which even a novice can cope with little practice.

Anchors such as the smaller Danforths fit snugly hanging over the after pulpit rail, most of the nylon cable stows neatly in the bottom of a large rubber bucket suspended outboard of the rail, while the inboard end of the nylon is led conveniently to a sheet winch. The length of chain, which goes out first with the anchor, is in the top of the bucket on top of the nylon. It is easy for the boat to move forwards and approach her berth with the anchor bitten in while the helmsman gently controls the boat's forward movement with the nylon round a sheet winch. His engine will be going steadily ahead, holding the nylon taut, and the slipstream from his screw will be acting on the rudder, even when the boat is nearly stopped, so that she still steers. This way it is possible to position the boat almost within an inch, and in almost any weather.

When leaving, the smaller boat avoids the problems of a larger boat leaving stern first. The large boat which has to weigh by power windlass is not under control while the cable comes slowly in. The smaller boat can coil down the lightweight nylon in the bucket with great speed.

There is always a problem anchoring in crowded Med harbours using a cable of taut nylon. The cable is at a very easy angle to the surface of the water, making it many yards out before the cable is deep enough for the keels (and the screws, which is worse) of manoeuvring boats to pass clear over it. In crowded harbours, therefore, be prepared to fit a weight on the nylon cable to hold it down. We have seen a nylon cable with a lead core, which seems a good idea, but we have never tried it.

The compensating disadvantage of bows-to (that it is more difficult to leave) is partially overcome by using very long scope on the anchor cable; what you must avoid while leaving is coming to a stop in order to break out the anchor from the bottom while the bow is still entangled with the anchor cables of other boats. Breaking out the anchor can be difficult; one can be inhibited from using the screw to 'motor out the anchor' because your own cable is right beside the screw, and so the breaking-out has to be done by main force – a difficult vertical pull in all but small boats if you do not have a powered after anchor windlass, though one should be able to get a lead to a sheet winch.

Another point to consider is that a less active person has more trouble boarding and leaving a yacht via the bows; we have seen some desperate struggling over the bows of the flotilla and bare-boat charter yachts that consistently moor this way. It is much easier for someone with limited mobility to use a gangway over the stern, especially in the bigger boats.

Bows-to is, in our opinion, easier to achieve than stern-to for boats up to 35 feet. From 35 to 45 it is arguable, from 45 upwards it is likely that stern-to will be easier, taking account of all the factors.

The stern-to option

Berthing stern-to seems to bring out a crisis of nervousness in some folk, but it is not difficult if approached correctly. The first thing to do is to discover the necessary speed astern to have full steerage. In a flat calm this will be quite slow. In a cross wind it might be fast enough to give some misgivings at first. Practise it somewhere where there is plenty of room and make notes of the results.

The secret is to back into the berth at the minimum speed to provide steerage in the prevailing conditions, and to go right in without stopping, at least until you are within reach of the quay. The moment you hesitate or stop, steerage way is lost, and you will be lucky to recover it if it is windy (it follows that a competent anchorman is an asset). While obviously not recommending that a skipper should plough on regardless into the next-door boat, if you have steerage way it is possible to steer her astern into the hole as long as you do not slow down; if you slow down too much you lose control over the directional movement of the boat. If you have made a mistake, or misjudged things and have to stop, then go straight out ahead and start all over again. You may think you are looking an idiot, but that is better than being a perpetrator of nautical carnage. Those who know anything about seamanship will respect you, and who cares what the rest think? It is no use having a boat if you cannot tolerate looking a proper charlie in front of the ignorant now and then. Ignore the tapping foot of the waiter who came to take your line, in the hope of hooking you into his establishment for the evening. Go round again. We once did it three times, in front of a reception committee, too. One has to moderate one's expectations.

Most of the accidents while berthing are caused by failure to anticipate events, leading to panic action. Try to decide a normal berthing policy and practise it, and then, because circumstances are never ideal, decide if and how this has to be modified before committing yourself to proceed. Then, skippers, try to explain in advance to the mate exactly what you intend to do. Misunderstandings between the crew lead to unnecessary difficulties, to the skipper losing his cool, his aim, and his judgement, and the crew picking up the same feeling. Even if heart attack is avoided the atmosphere does not lend itself to efficiency or contentment. Quite apart from the spectacle of a skipper gently reprimanding his crew at the top of his voice, because of his own lack of foresight or skill, and the visibly risible effect this has on spectators, it lowers the efficiency of everyone on board and must contribute to accidents.

Yachts *ought* to steer well when motoring astern because they all have to be berthed, and designers should take this into account. Unfortunately most have no idea of the desirable characteristics to achieve this facility in single-screw vessels. We can only advise having a trial sail and insisting on trying some berthing stern-to if this is the way that suggests itself for the boat you have in mind. There is nothing you can do about a boat with bad reversing characteristics after you have bought it, except sell it again (See also Heaving-to, page 105.)

Mooring stern-to provides simpler facilities for boarding. It is usually easier to rig a gangway and so be able to walk ashore. But again some yachts do not lend themselves to this convenience. Modern design fashion leans toward vulnerable vertical rudders deep-hung at the stern, where, as we have said, they damage themselves on the projecting underwater ballast of the quay, not to mention the accumulated detritus abandoned by Ulysses and his later compatriots, which you will be unable to see until after you have hit it.

Even then these rudders are more likely to pick up stray lines, anchor cables etc. from next-door boats who are not manoeuvring well. For real peace of mind a rudder well tucked out of the way is best. Boats with deep-hung rudders right aft end up berthed with their sterns well away from the quay, and need long gangways.

There is also a fashion for retroussé transoms, which leaves the deck even further from the quay. We are at a loss to understand how designers can consider boats 'ideal for cruising' with smooth, unbroken retroussé transoms. The retroussé stern is greatly improved if the 'retroose' is hollow, like a sugar scoop; in these circumstances it can be a positive feature, for, with steps down to the lower level we have a convenient ·bathing platform as well as good boarding from low quays. The 'retroose' also makes a good sea stowage for fenders which are bulky and otherwise clutter the deck, and also for cans of petrol if you carry an outboard motor. But then think of all that extra lazaret locker space you would have if there were a conventional transom!

Steps down the transom are a good idea in any boat. More conveniently done down a retroussé stern, a little ingenuity can usually arrange something for almost any stern except a counter stern. If you have a bolted-on ladder, have a hinged portion which can be lowered down to ease climbing out of the water when swimming, voluntarily or otherwise.

Stern gantries

A stern gantry is a sort of soccer goalpost erected transversely across the transom. It needs to have clearance headroom, and on top of it should go, for example, radar aerials, wind generators, solar panels (these can form a sort of mini-awning over the after end of the cockpit), GPS or Loran aerials, and other HF radio aerials. VHF aerials

The stern gantry. This is a rare example of a little ship thoughtfully fitted out as a retirement home, and it has many commendable features. The stern gantry carries most of the electronic junk as well as supporting davits for a tender and for a stern gangway. There is a convenient barbecue for those lovely warm evenings.

and anemometers are best placed higher up. Anything mounted on the gantry is far more accessible for working on than when up the mast, and does not interfere with the wind in the sails. The gear on the gantry will have lower centres of gravity than if mounted up the mast. On the gantry's after side it could carry the hoists/guys that control the gangway when it is down. Using these one does not have to unrig the gangway to leave harbour, as it can be simply and easily triced up to the gantry, where it is quite secure and out of the way.

The gantry can also provide service as a boom gallows, and can support a good awning. It is a convenience in any cruising yacht, but more important for our purposes, it saves a lot of awkward lifting and heaving. Some gantries are combined with stern davits which can be very useful.

Stern davits

The stern davits make sense. It is far better to have the dinghy out of the water while passage-making. And an inflatable dinghy hung on stern davits makes a very effective fender against possible trouble when berthed stern-to. It is not a use recommended by the makers, nor should it be a routine use, but things do happen to boats berthed end on to the quay: a sudden change and increase in wind, a larger boat berthing alongside and not doing it very well, or a departing neighbour dislodging your anchor while you are not there to adjust and re-set it. We know several yachtsmen who hang a canvas protector over the dinghy and let the inflatable take the strain.

Getting a load on board

It is important to have a means of lifting on board heavy weights. Examples are replacement batteries or full gas bottles. There are several possible approaches to this problem. If alongside, it is comparatively easy: a main boom can be used as a derrick, or failing that a tackle to a mast head halyard can lift while lateral movement is controlled from alongside. If end-on to the quay it is a different matter, and we have seen young and old struggling frantically to lift enormous weights over a bow pulpit. It is even worse sometimes if loading a dinghy; unless you think *that* exercise through prudently it can be a disaster. After being rationed to a can of beer per man per day on a transatlantic crossing, we almost lost a crate of it (more precious than rubies) during its transfer from dock to dinghy in a heavy swell in Barbados.

We have a light derrick pivoted at the foremast tabernacle (near the deck), which is long enough to plumb out over the bows. It is not only useful for loading but it is an effective way of weighing the anchor if the power winch breaks down. It can hoist long lengths of chain up at one time, and it also serves as a bearing-out spar for the jib.

Let us examine the potential trouble spots we mentioned earlier.

Boarding and leaving the boat

This is one of the areas requiring some agility. Circumstances where you can alight or board your boat easily from a simple alongside position on to a quay at exactly the same height as the freeboard of the boat are as rare as a Dutch mountain. They exist mostly on inland waterways and in some yacht clubs, but are seldom found when cruising. Throughout the Mediterranean one is usually berthed end on to a very low quay, as the tidal range is only about a foot. In the Caribbean one is nearly always at anchor and therefore going ashore by dinghy.

The Levkas pulpit. This illustrates quite a good stemhead arrangement. The short, flat bowsprit with its open-ended pulpit makes good access over the bows. Note the roller sheaves for two bower anchor cables. But just look at those sharp-edged 'fairleads'.

The half-Levkas pulpit. It has a lowered crossbar but you can see that it wouldn't be very easy to climb over it.

In some tidal harbours a kind of nautical mountaineering is necessary to climb up the quay at low tide, when the rusty old iron ladder is all hung about with seaweed, and seemingly a mile high.

Boarding over the bow is made difficult by the design of most pulpits, but the Levkas fore-pulpit helps to overcome this. It comes in several forms. At its simplest it consists of fixed rails on either side with no cross-member joining the two. Obviously like this it is not so strong, but it can be made strong enough. Some forms put a lower cross-member half way up, which gives it some lateral strength, though it means that the crew board or disembark through a U-shaped opening that is about a foot above the deck. A better form in our view is to have a hinged cross-member that folds back in harbour. These usually have to be specially made.

Even with an open Levkas pulpit, boarding over the bows is sometimes not easy. The stem of the boat is often higher than the stern, and quays (and marina pontoons) can be very low, perhaps only a few inches above the water. When made fast, a short ladder can be rigged depending from the overhanging stem, but when berthing, especially if there is no one on shore to take the first headrope, and with a strong wind blowing causing the stem to quest about like a Dalek's proboscis, there is an inevitable tendency to jump ashore in order to avert damage to neighbours or to one's own boat. This is not helped by the skipper, aft, hauling up on the anchor cable in a last-minute panic to stop the stem hitting the quay, a procedure that always causes the boat to spring backwards away from the quay like a puppy on a lead whose master has just noticed the little animal sniffing a wasp. The skipper will, of course, do this just as the crew tries to climb down with the headrope.

The only solution to this problem of getting ashore for'ard that we have found is to have fixed steps down the stem, or a fixable ladder forward, down which the crew can climb. Steps down the stem would only work for a boat with a near-vertical stem, and with current fashion these are rare.

We have a vertical stem and find it a great asset. It is very convenient to put it against the quay with a bow fender, and with the engine left going ahead we lean on the country we are visiting while we see to mooring ropes in slow time, clambering down via the rubbing strake and the anchor. Only boats with strong stems, though, usually steel ones, lend themselves to this treatment. We are beginning to notice that other people are using the bower anchor as a step. There is food for thought here, but one must avoid the wobble factor. A Swedish single-hander had a good solution to the problem of leaning his bows against the quay; see illustration.

On the other hand, there is no reason why a simple ladder about three feet (1 m) long cannot be rigged on one side or other of the stem in most boats. Possibly a side-boarding ladder could adapt and double in this role; it is something the ingenuity of the individual can achieve, but do avoid rope ladders; they are very dangerous for the non-athletic, unless they are properly tensioned.

Even when berthed alongside there is still the problem of boarding a boat which can be several feet above (or even below) the quay, especially if she is moving up or down a foot or two in the wash of a passing ferry. A ladder is more or less essential in any boat cruising in tidal waters. It can double as a boarding/swimming ladder.

If you are planning to berth stern-to then have proper facilities built in for a stout brow or gangway. Do not tolerate dangerous lash-ups. It must be light, though strong. It should have a twin-axis swivel at the boat end, so that it can be swung horizontally, as well as canted up or down. There should be a means of lifting the gangway's outer end from inboard (a tackle to a gantry is ideal, but a tackle to a halyard or to stern davits will do) so that it is just clear of the ground. On some boats one sees a gangway with little wheels or even casters. These are to take up the movements caused by the boat surging in her berth, as otherwise the end of the gangway would wear out. They are not so good in a small boat where the gangway is light weight and has less

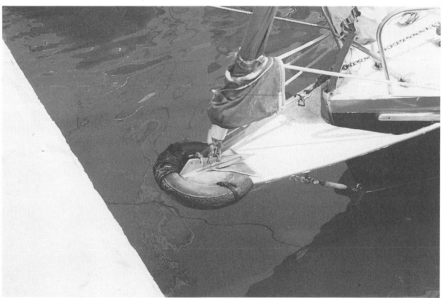

These two photographs illustrate the way in which an elderly Swedish single-hander solved the problem of berthing bows-to in his small yacht. Note the old tyre fixed to the stem rail which could take the strain while the boat leant against the quay.

inertia; they have the potential for moving underfoot like a skate-board, and this is dangerous. We have no wheels on ours but hoist it up a few inches above the ground using stretchable nylon line, and stay it so it does not wobble about. The weight of someone stepping on to the gangway puts it firmly on the ground, and when they get off it, it springs up an inch or two clear. The first few times one steps off can be a little disconcerting but one soon gets accustomed. Of course, this would not be of any use in tidal waters.

We have solid wooden handrails at the sides of our gangway; the flimsy rope dangling between miniature stanchions represents false security, though it is helpful if it is only balance that is a problem.

Some purchasable gangways have the tread part made of handsome teak gratings. They look very smart indeed. Unfortunately the holes are just the right size to trap the end of one's walking stick. If you use a stick, even if only occasionally, wooden gratings are not recommended, except perhaps in the shower.

Apologia

On reading this chapter through carefully we felt we might be accused of concentrating too much on the problems as relating to the Mediterranean. What answer do we have?

Bill has arrived by sea in 94 different countries, all over the world, and firmly believes that the most suitable cruising grounds for older folk lie in non-tidal waters such as the Med, especially the eastern part, and in the Intracoastal Waterway of the USA. Already there are innumerable old folk cruising these areas, more than in the rest of the world put together (our estimate). We plan to gravitate to one or other, or perhaps both, as our faculties atrophy. Practically everything we have written about the Med is applicable to the ICW, but not necessarily vice versa. We think our emphasis is valid.

Fending off

Much of what we have already written above has to do with berthing. Accidents and mishaps often occur in fending off or in jumping ashore in a hurry. Fending should only be done with fenders, never with feet or fingers.

We have never been able to understand the growing tendency to protect one's fenders. Soon we will need fender-buskins to protect the fender-socks to protect the fenders that protect the ship. Let the fenders take the strain. They only need hanging there, but this supposes a certain amount of intelligent anticipation in getting them to the right place. Fixed length lanyards tied to dedicated eyes are not appropriate, they never cope with all the sizes and shapes of the boats or quays you might be up against. In passing, have the fender lanyards made of floating rope. One does drop fenders over the side from time to time, and one wants to minimise the chances of the lanyard being sucked into the screw, thus disabling the ship.

The ideal fenders for steel boats, particularly on canals, are old motor tyres, which can be painted white with two coats of chlorinated rubber paint if you wish to avoid black stains. If you want to use tyres, and there is really nothing better for hard wear and tear, then beware of getting them too large and therefore heavy. It is essential to drill a drainage hole in them, otherwise the weight of collected water becomes more than one should lift. Mini tyres are best as they are easily moved around. Note that tyre fenders are illegal on canals in France unless fitted with inner tubes or filled with foam so that they will float if they come adrift, and not sink down to jam up the lock gates.

Cooking
Cooking as a potential source of accidents is dealt with in Chapter 13.

Aloft
Oddly enough, going aloft is not so much of a problem for older folk. They have more sense than the young monkeys who are up and down the masts like Tarzan among the tree trunks; they go up only when there is a demonstrable need to do so, and defer it if possible until the conditions are ideal. Bill no longer climbs masts without a bosun's chair. He no longer hauls himself up, but relies on the hydraulic windlass to do it for him. He does not try to do too much at a time, though there is an argument that as one stays up and gets adapted to life in space, the muscles relax and work becomes easier. If there is anything complex or energetic to do up there, Bill now waits until refit time and elicits the help of a fit young ally from another boat. In the yottie community there are always some who are running short of cash, and we took advantage of this recently to have our three wooden masts painted.

Accidents aloft have been caused by fainting, and by losing one's grip. Bill has personal experience of the former caused by climbing *Fare Well*'s mast steps when he was feeling very unwell already, an inherently stupid thing to do. He had, as always, clipped on his safety harness, but fell the full length of its lanyard. Laurel then had the job of disentangling 200 lbs of deadweight captain hanging halfway down the mast. Not an easy task, but with help she did it and he was lowered to the deck, where she brought him round by throwing water and abuse at him.

The adrenalin surges while in unusual and potentially dangerous places and one's blood pressure rises in these risky circumstances.

With high adrenalin one acts instinctively, and often without careful thought. Life is easier if the work can be done at deck level, and it can if the masts are in tabernacles, an elementary and simple way of stepping masts that we would strongly recommend for every cruising boat. It saves money if you can raise and lower your own masts without help, and you can work on the rigging without climbing.

Another structural precaution is not to have steps up the mast, thus avoiding the temptation to climb them. Do, however, have a pair of steps, one each side at equal height, about three feet below the truck, or any other point where you might conceivably have to spend some time on maintenance. This is because a feeling of insecurity when you are 60 feet above the deck increases your tension, is tiring and distracting, and is the indirect cause of accidents. Insecurity is increased as one dangles about, swinging from side to side as the boat moves. A passing motor-boat can cause a lot of anguish. The ability to brace one's feet on two firm steps, and to have one's waist or chest secured to a strong point by a good harness, gives a stability that enables one to work with two hands and get the job done in a quarter of the time before you tire. It also by happy chance gives you the opportunity to make rude gestures to passing craft who have not slowed down, and who would otherwise have interrupted your work. Do not, however, overindulge yourself with rude gestures if you are not fully secured, and especially not with the hand that you are holding on with.

Rough seas

Choppy conditions at sea make one's balance and foothold more chancy. The worst, in our opinion, is not the very rough sea, when to move at all requires careful thought, but the slight chop which will have the boat moderately steady for a minute or so, and then roll her ten degrees or slam her into a wave without any warning. It can happen even in calm weather if you happen to pass a fast-going big ship, or one of these modern breeds of motor cruiser that seem to be designed to cause the maximum wash. With these latter you usually get some warning; most have their engines virtually unsilenced and go their brutal way about the seas making a noise like a Boeing taking off. It is the sudden and unexpected that knocks the pot off the stove and scalds the cook ... That traps the navigator just when he is using both hands on his parallel ruler and does not have his feet braced ... That tumbles you head down into a floor locker or tips you bodily into the bilge. All these have happened to us, and two of them happened in harbour! It is inconsiderate drivers we are against rather than motor boats *per se*; there are, as we well know, careful motor-boating people.

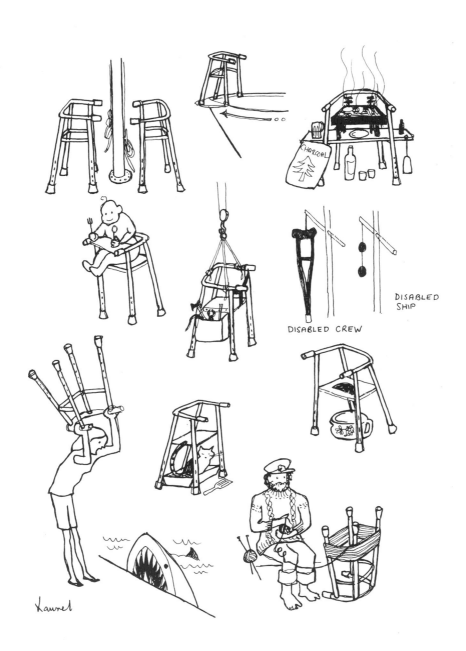

Uses of a zimmer frame on board.

Prevention of accidents

The problem is that these accidents happen because the factors that cause them are unexpected, and it is difficult to maintain alertness to every risk all the time. Prevention has to be by built-in means that minimise the results of the problem. Fitting the navigator's throne with arms may stop him falling out of it, but it also makes it difficult to wriggle into, especially if wearing foul-weather gear. There is not a lot that you can do about falling into bilge lockers except make them less deep; if you make their openings smaller you risk getting your head or shoulders stuck, leaving you with your feet sticking out like Pooh Bear in the rabbit hole. Every solution is a bit of a compromise.

For risks of this nature it is necessary to look carefully at the interior of the boat and then fit grabrails wherever they suggest themselves, for the builder will not have done it for you, or at least not as many as may be desirable. If the boat is in other ways satisfactory, take a half dozen or so good strong handholds together with their screws so that you can fit them where experience indicates their need. That way you do not fall into the same locker twice. If fixing to thinnish plywood (under 20 mm), bolts backed up with oversize washers on the back are desirable fastenings. We do not think there is any need to go on about handholds, lifelines and so on. It is mostly common sense. But do see that guardrails are strong and high. Accept a little less elegance in the boat's profile to have them really high, but if you are considering replacing the low stanchions already fitted by longer ones, be very careful that the fastenings to the deck are man enough for the extra strains that will be caused by forces exerted at the tops of the raised rails.

If it is necessary to go to the foot of the mast to attend to halyards, then have stout 'granny-rails' round the mast. These are a sort of pulpit either side of the mast, that can take care of you if you lose your footing while pulling strings. They should be three feet (1 m) high and be braced athwartships. They make good places to hang spare lashings, shackles, and other handy bits.

There should be a new approach to moving around the deck in choppy seas. Some of our acquaintances who are defying age in many respects, and who have done so by great prudence, tell us that they habitually move about the deck on all fours at sea. One of them, an octogenarian, shuffles on his bottom, an excellent idea as you have a fifth point of contact with the deck (there would still be three if both hands are in use), and this method keeps your centre of gravity low. He says he has non-slip soles to his shoes, but finds it difficult to so equip the back of his shorts. He should try the padding material that protects polished tables from scorch-marks. Good for knees, too.

One does not wish to take a tumble into the guardrails in rough weather. One can hit stanchions with a lot of damaging force, possibly carrying them away, or one can go over the top. Boatbuilders, presumably to save a penny or two, persistently fit guardrails, cleats, bitts, eyes, and grabrails that are suitable only for fairy boats. Even if they appear stout enough, be sure they are adequately fastened. With many of today's production boats fastenings of deck-fittings are hidden behind fancy difficult-to-remove linings and cannot easily be checked. If the boat is being built for you then the builder will usually be prepared to up-grade the fastenings, but even if he is willing it is necessary to check personally – the willingness may not have been communicated to the workman who actually does the job.

In passing it should be noted that many of the workmen and production engineers in the modern boat factories are not trained shipwrights, and they have little idea of the strains and uses of what they fit. This was brought home to us when a joiner who did a job for us aboard *Fare Well* removed one of the four bolts of a heavy piece of machinery in order to 'Get a better fair-in' with his woodwork. If we had not noticed, the whole machine could have come adrift in a seaway. They work to orders, or occasionally their own short cuts, which might well have originated in the shop-fitting trade. The real shipwright is in a dying trade; he works too carefully for modern production-line methods. These furniture factory work practices (which are more evident in certain French boat-building companies than in British or Dutch yards) cause us concern. One can, and usually has to, take a new motor-car back to the local agent to correct dozens of things that might be wrongly adjusted. You cannot easily do that when your boat is already at sea. What one may call warranty boatyards are found here and there, inconspicuous centres where the 'Monday products' of the boat factories of Finland and France can be cobbled into usable condition.

Tenders

A brief word about tenders. First is the desirability of hoisting them inboard while on passage. Though towing a dinghy is quite practicable on many occasions, it is when things go wrong that it becomes a pest. It is well known that things never go wrong in isolation, mishaps almost always occur in threes. If the third thing happens before you have coped with the second, and the second before you have coped with the first, why, then you are in a spot of bother. By having the dinghy safely inboard one source of trouble is out of the way. One classic mishap that arises when towing a dinghy occurs when berthing stern-to. The dinghy is taken to the bows to clear the stern for backing into the narrow berth. The bowman, watching the skipper for the signal to let go the anchor does so exactly when told, and the anchor drops neatly into the dinghy...

To stow the tender on deck means that there must be an easy, effortless way of getting it there. We have watched inflatables, first emptied of removable gear, and then with their painters shackled to a halyard, being hoisted up the mast to be subsequently lowered safely to the deck. Not a bad system except that it is neccesary to unship the outboard. (See our injunctions about lifting weights.) There is also the following unhappy chance (we have admittedly seen it only once): the yacht was hoisting the inflatable to get all secure for leaving the anchorage in a hurry, and had it well up her foremast when she was hit by a violent squall. The dinghy flew off horizontally like a kite, but was unbalanced and danced about at the end of its 'kite-string', wrapping itself in and around everything it could find. It was a terrible distraction for the helmsman, and the yacht went aground.

We think side davits are the best, but they are really practical only on largish yachts; failing them, then stern davits are good. Though some say that the hoisted dinghy is still in a vulnerable position in rough following seas, we have never heard of damage to a dinghy caused this way. If the stern davits are associated with a gantry, they are that much higher than if fitted to the deck.

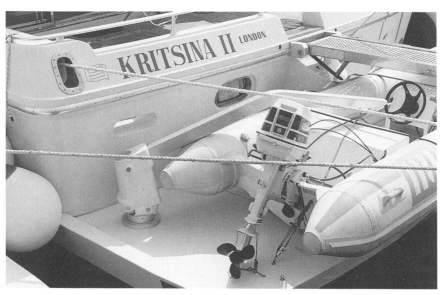

A miniature hydraulic crane. We have been looking for a sea-going version of this for a long time and this is the only one we have seen – aboard a rather luxurious Italian-built motor yacht. Someone ought to make a less ritzy version for the cruising yacht.

Now that even quite small delivery vans have hydraulic hoists, surely someone could market a lightweight crane for medium sized cruising yachts. These hydraulic ones collapse like a dying swan when not in use; they would be an ideal accessory for sailors like us.

The vexed question of rigid versus inflatable tender will never be finally resolved, and must depend on personal preference. We prefer a rigid dinghy, but there are occasions when we rather wish we had an inflatable (usually when there is the necessity of leaving one's dinghy afloat in some harbour where the only available place is rocky and subject to the wash of passing craft). We believe most people feel this doubt in one direction or another. The only firm opinion we have here is that the dinghy should not be a miniature one in either case, for it should have some stability; if inflatable, it should have rigid flooring, and if a rigid dinghy, it should have reasonably horizontal bottom boards to minimise the chance of slipping as you board. Beware of clever folding dinghies, especially those resembling envelopes, unless you can face the prospect of them folding when you least expect them to, sticking down the flap, and posting you to Poseidon.

If you have an inflatable you are condemned to have an outboard. Perhaps you like these smelly, awkward, heavy, contrary, irritable, hernia-inducing monsters. (Do we make our feelings clear?) You are condemned, because inflatables cannot be easily rowed in a wind or sea of any strength. Nor can some rigid dinghies, usually those streamlined soapdish shaped plastic novelties, whose designers never tried rowing them. Choose one that can be rowed with ease (it will usually look like a boat), and make sure the oars are long enough, and have comfortable handgrips. The rowing does you good if you do it properly, and can be a pleasure. Better still, get a dinghy that has a sail as well.

Companionway ladders

Boarding a dinghy from a yacht is fraught with dangers. The elegant side ladder, with its platform at deck level and again just above the water line, is only really suitable for large yachts because the gear is only stable when heavy, and when braced at low level against the yacht's side. More usual in the size of yacht we are envisaging is what the Royal Navy call a Mediterranean Ladder, that is, a vertical ladder down the yacht's side. These should be stout, but not so heavy that you cannot lift them out easily. It is better if they extend underwater for three feet or so, to become swimming ladders if you should wish such a fitting. Ideally, they should have guys from low down on the ladder extending fore and aft, because tenders coming alongside tend to nudge the ladder. They also nudge the ladder if the sea happens to be a bit bouncy, and a person half way up can be discomfited thereby.

The retroussé stern can have a boarding ladder down its sloping face, as we have already pointed out. This has its disadvantages for boarding a dinghy because the dinghy has to lie at right angles to the yacht, and this can cause problems in a strong wind or tide.

Man overboard

Because it involves ship's gear, we will go into the subject here.

It is a sad truth that the elderly are much more liable to fall overboard, especially in harbour when their concentration may lapse. We base this partly on experience with Laurel's irrepressible mother Linet, who fell in frequently in her 50's and 60's, but got more careful in her 80's. It is also true that the elderly find it more difficult to extricate themselves from the situation we refer to as 'taking a voluntary', borrowing the expression from our cavalry friends.

Remember, above all, that it is extremely difficult, if not virtually impossible, for anyone, even when young and agile, to get back on board unaided, if the freeboard is high. The victim has had a shock, the water may be cold, and often they are not properly dressed for swimming. It might also be very difficult for the survivor left on board to hoist up a tired, shocked, heavy, dripping wet, helpless lump, bearing in mind that the hoister will him- or herself merit several of the above adjectives. In *Fare Well* we had ready means of hoisting anything out of the water with a side davit and an electric capstan. It was part of our planning. It was never used for a person, except to exercise the system, but it could have been. (We rescued sizeable logs, a crate of bananas, a sack of grapefruit, and innumerable beach balls.)

Another good and workable method is to use a masthead halyard, and to hoist up the victim on a halyard winch, though with roller furling these are getting rarer. It also drags the poor fellow over the gunwale, but a few minor bruises are not unacceptable in the interests of speed in these circumstances. When Bill fell overboard in his youth (we sailed without guardrails in those days) he was hauled, unconscious, into a rowing boat by the Royal Engineers Rowing Club, and sustained some nasty bruises to his ribs. He has never allowed these to detract in any way from his gratitude to all Sappers.

The chief problem is to get a good sling or harness on the casualty. If they are unconscious this is very difficult indeed without actually going into the water, and if the total crew is but two, you could be in trouble. (Most tumbles overboard happen in harbour, and most drownings also.)

Rig a swimming ladder and go down it far enough to slip a running bowline round the person's chest. It is better still to carry a proper sling; a sort of large loop with a fitting like a Boy Scout's woggle which can be pushed down the loop to hold the casualty in. This is much easier to slip over the head and make fast under the arms.

On deck we would like to see, even on quite small boats, a dedicated rope led over a dedicated sky-hook somewhere (whether davit, gantry, spreader arm, or whatever), and led by leading blocks to an electric winch or windlass with a warping drum. This use alone, in a boat for older people, justifies the expense of an electric windlass. Even if the casualty is fully conscious, and apparently unharmed, he will be far more tired than he thinks. And everyone on board, together with those who love you on shore, will be just that little bit easier in their minds that a dreadful possibility has been looked in the eye, and allowed for.

There are on the market several proprietory makes of sling for recovery of persons overboard. We have not seen a comparative review of them all, and therefore hesitate to make a recommendation. The one called 'Lifesling' seems to us to be workmanlike and practical. If any magazine would consider investigating these would they remember to look at them from an older person's point of view. If you do get one of these, then make sure it is suitable for lifting by helicopter.

Yacht designers

We have occasionally been less than polite about the designers of cruising yachts. It must be obvious that not all of them are bad at their job, for there are very many contented people cruising the world, and we assume that the designs of their boats are satisfactory. It is thus hard to generalise, and in a book of this nature that is just what one is obliged to do.

What we have observed is that boats built by famous designers of racing yachts are seldom good cruising yachts, no matter that they may be fun to sail. There is much more to cruising than sailing the boat.

A good cruising boat is a compromise of many functions. What is *not* a compromise is the so-called cruiser-racer, which has to be a sell-out in one direction or the other. If it wins, it is not a cruiser, if it loses it is not a racer. There are many examples of good cruising boat designers: to be positive therefore, let us mention the names Pape, Rock, Griffiths, Holman, Petersen, Rhodes, Alden. We also like an American boat called the Westsail, but do not know her designer. A Canadian boat called Vancouver designed by Robert Harris, deserves examination. There is a version of this modified by Kevin Seymour and others, the Vancouver Pilot built in England, which we thought a good cruising yacht with sensible gear. There are many others, so our apologies to any deserving souls we have omitted.

One problem remains when buying new yachts: the standard provision of gear is always hopelessly inadequate. The extra cost over and above the standard price before the yacht could be of any practical use might be enormous. Unless you already have a substantial amount of appropriate-sized gear to bring from another boat one should allow 20% extra for making a new yacht seaworthy.

12

A Word to the Women

Mary, Mary, *be* contrary,
Watch how your boat is growing:
Demand your bells and cockle shells,
Otherwise you're not going!

WE ARE A CERTAIN kind of woman, who go off cruising with our men for six months, sometimes the whole year. We are not special, we are not brave, we are not particularly adventurous, and we are all extremely different, but we do have a few qualities in common, and if you wish to head off oceanwards in retirement, it would be as well to consider whether you have those qualities. We went into them in depth in the *Sell Up and Sail* quiz to decide what your Ulysses Quotient was: your aptitude and abilities for a life of this kind (both you and your man) so we will merely summarise here what we observe to be common to cruising women:

- A large fund of commonsense.
- A practical approach to problems.
- A willingness to learn.
- An ability to assess what is needed, and do it.
- Reasonable accord and understanding with your spouse.
- Trust in his (and your) abilities.
- Understanding and acceptance of the other's weaknesses.
- A pioneering spirit.
- The will to go.

We are not:

- Plucky little chaps.
- Good girl scouts.
- Cooks and bottle washers.
- The little woman.
- Captain's comforts.

132

We are people with certain expectations (moderate, of course, at our age); we have our own norms and requirements, and they should be heeded if we are to take what for many women is a drastic step into unknown territory. It should not remain unknown. Opportunities must be taken to familiarise oneself with it. Choice must be based on knowledge. Do you like the sea, or would canals suit you better? Try them both.

When you have both decided which way is best to go, then you start thinking about the boat to do it in, and here again you must say your piece. Designers and manufacturers of boats are twenty years out of date with what a woman wants, and the only reason for that is that we do not speak up. The women who hit the headlines and make known their needs are usually the doers of doughty deeds in racing craft, who want the same kind of boat as the racing men; indeed they must have such a boat in order to be competitive. Yachting has been a man's world for centuries, and old habits die hard. In some countries where 'yachting' is still six chaps and a filthy galley these habits are not dying at all. We cruising wives cannot expect attention from the media except in shipwreck or piracy, but it is time our voice was heard by designers and boatyards. We have mentioned the Moody Owners' Association, where at last the wives are having their say, to some effect. Perhaps we are only allowed a say in small things as yet, furnishings, galley details, and ease of bedmaking; but soon we might change the thinking behind the actual design of the boat, and yank the designers back to cruising sense instead of racing fashions.

To do that needs informed and firm opinions, otherwise some young sprig of a salesman at a boat show will be whispering to your chap: 'I don't think Madam has quite understood the problem'. Madam also is buying this boat, and Madam understands her own problems very well. We are a bit beyond having our little heads patted and being told to go and play while the big boys talk business. If we are going to spend even six months of the year in a boat, of which we are probably part-owner, it is very much our business if the venture is to be the success that everyone (even with moderate expectations) dreams of.

It has long been common knowledge among stockbrokers that women are the owners of a large majority of the privately owned ordinary shares quoted on the Stock Exchange. Some research into the small and larger Ship Registries would reveal, we suggest, some statistics that could upset the marketing philosophy of the yachting industry. (If the research extended into ages of owners, the results could be of earthquake dimensions.) Our sample poll of part of the register indicates that well over half the boats over 35 feet are owned by people over 55, and that there are as many women among the names as men.

To retire successfully into a cruising boat requires much hard work beforehand. From what we have already said, you will realize that it would be a mistake to leave it all to your bloke, or you will not get the kind of boat you will be happy in. There are many solo ancient mariners sailing the seas in leaky boats with hard bunks and damp cabin soles, no heat, one oil lamp, and an austere diet of corned beef and cocoa. They are as happy as a pig in the mire, but they *are* solo. If you want to go too, then you should both aim for a comfortable ride, and come to some compromise on the kind of boat you want and the sort of travelling you will do. If working together like this tells you nothing else, it will test your ability to get on with each other in different circumstances from your previous life.

PART FOUR

Don't Shoot the Albatross
(It's Doing Its Best)

13

Treat Yourself Kindly

Jack and Jill are sailing still
They love to be out on the water
But if Jack falls down and breaks his crown
His cruising days will be shorter.

Health and happiness in boats

We make no promises, but have observed that sailing keeps you young, or at least enables you to ignore your age, which is nearly as good. (Though, as Chevalier said: 'Old age isn't so bad when you consider the alternative.') We have lost count of the number of young sailors we meet sailing with their grandchildren (whether round the buoys on the reservoir, or Spitzbergen and back in the Christmas holidays, is merely a matter of degree). We notice that on balance the longer the cruise the more your stress disorders are discarded.

Sailing is potent medicine. It can magic away your asthma and migraine, and you can wave goodbye to hay fever. It won't quite rid you of your wooden leg or battery bypass, but when you are sailing you are too busy to notice them, which is almost the same thing. There is nothing like a happily occupied mind and body to push your ailments into the background. Who has not sat forlorn at home with the mother and father of a cold, steeped in misery and menthol, then, when jollied along to the Kings Arms by good friends has forgotten all ills and jugged up and sung along with the rest?

Everyone knows that sea cruises were prescribed in the old days to get you over whatever ailed you, from gout to an unsuitable love affair. You sat in your deckchair, breathing in the ozone, your slightest whim your steward's command, and recovered your health, your equilibrium, and your senses during the long lazy sunny days at sea. Are cruises on small boats like a cruise on the pre-war *Mauretania*?. Well, not in all respects. You get the ozone, the sun (if you pick the right spot and season) and the view (often). You may get relaxation and good food and drink, but the whims are inclined to be those of the mate, and if he/she feels like doing bacon butties rather than a rib roast and apple pie, then bacon butties you will get. You will occasionally get unlooked-for bad weather as well, or An Unpleasant Experience while Berthing. Still, eating your butties while the sun shines on a blue sea, with a gentle wind in the right direction, an escort of dolphins, and the mountains of your target island faint in the distance, what could be better for your wellbeing? We do not have to go that far, unless we wish to. A gentle dinghy sail out on the lake to have a picnic on a fine day is also restoring to the equilibrium.

And suppose the cruise is one of those memorable for what went wrong? Not what the doctor ordered, in fact. The weather was bad, the boat unready, the crew fratchy, Grannie fell off her motor bike, your dinghy capsized?

One could paraphrase Biggles:

> *If you encounter bad weather, one of two things will happen: either the boat will sink, or it will not. If it does not, there is no need to worry.*
>
> *If the boat sinks, one of two things will happen: either you will be rescued, or you will not. If you are rescued, there is no need to worry.*
>
> *If you are not rescued, one of two things will happen: either you will survive, or you will not. If you survive, there is no need to worry.*
>
> *If you do not, you won't be able to worry …*

Contrariwise, in the real world, there is a good deal to worry about. For heaven's sake, worry constructively.

How to worry constructively
Do everything you can beforehand to prevent your bad dreams coming true. This goes right back to choosing the boat, learning what you need to know (and ensuring that your partner and/or crew know it too), sizing up your capabilities and recognizing your shortcomings, and providing for them. The process continues by keeping the boat (and yourselves) properly maintained, equipping your boat (and yourselves) with care, and planning your journeys with forethought and a good eye on the weather.

We all, in spite of this, get caught out sometime and undergo a bad experience. Most of us come through. Be honest: you do not often see the headline: 'Octogenarian Lost at Sea' but it is surprising how many of them there are out there, sailing the oceans. So, you got through. You have learnt a great deal from the experience. You have a sense of achievement, even pride. You may be looking at your partner with new and wondering eyes, since he or she may have turned out to be an ace at fire-fighting, head bandaging, hashslinging in bad weather, or able to keep a cool head even after everyone else stopped being cool because they had suddenly realised what was happening. You solved problems and took decisions (even saying 'Well, we can't do anything about *that*' is a decision), and the stimulation received by your grey cells will probably keep them from stultifying for the next ten years.

On the whole, then, sailing is a rewarding and rejuvenating way of life. It is good for you. It is non-polluting. It is non-invasive. It breaks no laws and offends no one. It is decorative. (The sight of a fleet of sailing boats on sparkling blue water from a viewpoint such as Sherley Heights in Antigua is unforgettable; I hope it is an image that will stay stamped on my brainscreen for the rest of my life.)

However, accidents occur on boats as they do at home; illnesses may be contracted, some condition that you thought was under control may suddenly worsen. Even falling in the water is not such a light matter at our age. A little thought beforehand can save a lot of anguish. We will give a plan of campaign for healthy sailing into a ripe old age, with a few items that the young would probably not find necessary in their medical kit.

Health insurance

This should be thought of if your cruise is likely to last longer than a month. It has to be said that it is expensive. Worth the money in peace of mind if you can afford it, but if you can afford it, you can probably also afford to be ill without it. Like much insurance of this kind, if this is what you want you should have started sooner: a policy-holder with a good record going way back will pay a lot less than a new proposer. The underwriter will ask himself, 'Why is he starting insurance now?' Underwriters are the most suspicious persons on earth; they believe everyone is exercising an option against them. Sometimes they are right.

There are specialist brokers who can advise on health insurance for long-distance travellers. After all, so many of us now are ballooning over Baffin Island, or cycling through the outback, that cruising for six months in the Eastern Mediterranean seems a fairly mild undertaking in comparison. But beware; all these policies are annual contracts and the company can always decide not to renew and there is nothing you can do about it. Very often they decide to do just that, perhaps when you have made a claim, or when you need them most. Or else they exclude the illness that you are most likely to get.

No health insurance?

Commonsense is necessary. If you want to cruise in the US where medical expenses are high you would do well to have insurance. However, if your parents and grandparents died full of years, and you are basically healthy, you may not need insurance in Europe. There reciprocal agreements exist with the NHS, and you can usually get good treatment, which in some countries (France and Holland for example) you will pay for and reclaim later.

An alternative, or supplement, to insurance is the body known as MASTA (Medical Advisory Services for Travellers Abroad) which provides you, for a fee, with a Health Brief to your individual requirements, and a list of medical items to take with you. The address will be found in the appendix.

We considered consulting a gerontologist to advise us on this section of the book, and after some thought decided that such a specialist was just what we did not need, since if we are thinking about sailing into old age we are obviously far from senile, moderately healthy and have an optimistic outlook. What we need is advice to enable us to stay that way as long as possible. The best person to give you this advice is, oddly enough, yourself. At our age, we ought to know what ails us better than the doctor; if you have lived with your body for sixty-odd years or more no-one knows it better than you do. No-one knows its strengths and weaknesses, and what to do about them, as you do. Now is the time to take a bit more responsibility for your wellbeing. No one knows better than you what foods insult your gastric tract, what drinks are unkind to your intelligence and the brilliance of your nose, and what sort of lifestyle suits the even tenor of your ways. No good clutching your hernia and saying 'I ought not to have hauled in that anchor.' We have to learn to say 'Sorry, I can't do that,' without sounding either wimpish or aggressive.

Listen to your body; it is telling you something. Pay attention. Understand what it wants. In the simplest terms, fatigue means it wants rest, and corns means it wants better fitting shoes, but it goes much deeper than this. You know the risks you run, by your family history. If your parents were still happily gardening into their eighties, you are not likely to have early heart trouble. Doctors come in handy to check these risks and cross them off the list, we hope. If not, then to explain how to manage them.

Fortunately, on your own boat you can ensure that you have the necessary aids to do the heavy work. You can adapt the boat to your needs, never yet addressed, as far as we know, by any commercial boatbuilder, though we have seen and admired many boats with loving provision made by their owners for their loyal but stiffjointed or disabled spouses, even to wheelchair access, the building-in of baths, and strong grabrails round the heads. You can learn that there is more than one way to do something that is getting too much for you. You can sail a little less and motor a little more if the weather is unkind. You can be a little less hard on yourself, and your crew, and go more for comfort and labour-saving devices than you once did.

A long distance boat to be healthy in

This will contain a few things that have not yet occurred to most naval architects, though they are to be found in custom-made boats, and those lovingly converted with particular disabilities in mind. (We should point out, before we get taken to task, that as a practising cripple Laurel has no patience with politically correct euphemisms. She finds nothing wrong with the word disabled.)

- Such a boat will have really good guardrails.
- It will be stable.
- There will be handholds wherever they are needed, and then a few more.
- Ladders and companionways will be easy to manage and with firm bannisters and non-slip treads.
- There will be a light, strong bathing ladder, or some other means of getting back on board easily, whether your swim was voluntary or not.
- Changes in height of the floor of the accommodation will be kept to a minimum.
- The bunks will be extremely comfortable and easy to make, even if you want to use sheets and blankets instead of a sleeping bag or duvet.
- The heads will be well designed and easy to clean. There will be handholds to assist when sitting or standing to perform one's material ablutions whatever they may be. The space will be adequate, so that elderly people can emerge from it with dignity, and not with both feet down one trouser leg. With a bit of luck the flushing system will be electric, since, as pumping gets harder, it tends to be skimped.
- There will be a bath, for reasons already stated or yet to come, failing that a deep shower tray with facilities for sitting in it.
- There will be efficient and user-friendly heating.
- There will be no part of the boat that is too dark to be safe at

night, ie; lamps will be frequent and sufficient, and fitted with double switches at each end of any passage or compartment with two exits. This gets complicated with fluorescent lights, which are voltage sensitive.

We go further than saying that there should be comfortable places to sit; *all* places to sit should have sitting headroom, be at the right height from the floor – how seldom this is the case, and how often are seats crammed into spaces that crick your neck, your back, and catch you under the knees with a rigid bar that gives you terminal pins and needles in ten minutes. Some of these sitting places should offer you the chance of putting your feet up, as well. When the weather gets bad, and you cannot avoid it, you will be glad if the helmsman's chair is well designed, so that you can sit comfortably for longish periods and not be thrown out of it if the boat lurches. Whoever is not steering will need a similarly comfortable 'bad weather corner'; we sometimes think that seat-belts could be a good idea in cockpits of small boats. The usual method of sitting athwartships and bracing one's feet on the opposite bench blocks everyone else's passage and is very tiring to the calf and ankle muscles. A favourite spot is to sit fore and aft on the lee cockpit seat with one's feet up and one's back firmly against the bulkhead, if the construction allows, but a roll lands you on the cockpit floor. Seat-belts would prevent this.

The above requirements at present make most boat designers reel and think in terms of eighty-foot yachts. Not so. We have seen these features in thirty-footers. (Not all at once, it is true.) It is just going to need a different kind of thinking. There are a hell of a lot of ancient mariners, there ought to be a hell of a market for such a cruising boat.

A–Z of staying well

We will concentrate on prevention of illness and staying well on your cruise, rather than attempt an encyclopaedic What to Do Till the Doctor Rows Across.

Long before you go, have a good talk with your doctor. (Choose one that knows what sailing involves, however.) Make sure that you can manage your afflictions while you are afloat. Know how to use the drugs he gives you, what side effects there might be, and how often you should be checked up on. An honest look at any future symptoms that ought to be seen to would be good, but some doctors fear that the very idea of these might cause you to imagine that you had them. A sailing doctor, of course, realizes that at sea we are all far too busy to imagine symptoms; the problem is usually the opposite one: we cannot remember where we acquired that spectacular bruise.

Coleridge's Ancient Mariner brought ill fortune to his shipmates by shooting an albatross. Repenting, he walks the earth with a green message – live in harmony with all God's creatures.

Accidents

Avoid them. Think ahead, move with care, hold on, wear nonslip shoes which are properly fastened. In bumpy weather wear a padded jacket (the kind with built-in inflatable life jacket and safety harness) not just in case of falling overboard, but to cushion the bruises and prevent broken bones. Respect the forces involved in sailing even small boats in a strong wind, use the right machinery to avoid pushing or pulling, ie blocks and winches and fenders.

It is astonishing how many six-foot gorillas throw Laurel ropes and expect her to pull their boat, all ten tons of it, into the quay, or alongside *Hosanna*. Never fall for this one; make the rope fast to something strong and let the youngsters do the pulling. If something large is approaching your boat, do not try to stop it with any part of your body. Whether it is the quay or another boat, insert a fender at the right spot. Intelligent use of fenders is something we are all capable of, and can save us from severe injury. We are finding some of our bigger tyres too heavy for quick action now; what one needs in these circumstances is something large, light, and strong, like the balloon fender we have recently purchased.

The second most frequent cause of injury on boats is jamming one's fingers in something. The modish black fingernail Laurel sports at present got trapped in one of her kitchen drawers.

The third cause is probably banging one's head, either ducking down a hatchway or catching the boom as it goes across. Many people wear the caps known as Breton fishermen's, which are well padded. Some even wear hard hats.

Aches and pains

Rheumatism, arthritis, stiff joints, frozen shoulders, we are all as we get older subject to this sort of muscular and skeletal pain on occasions. Your doctor will prescribe something suitable, but think how comforting a hot bath is. More and more boats, even quite small ones, are finding the space for a tub just a bit bigger and deeper than a shower tray. With strong handles to aid getting in and out and an economical method of heating the water (which can be sea water, see Baths in Chapter 9) a warm bath is beneficial, has no side effects and brings with it the heavenly possibility of combining it with drinking a medicinal slug of what you fancy... small treats like this are a godsend until conditions improve. (The bath might have to wait till later.)

Antibiotics

It is as well to know that in many foreign parts these are freely available over the counter. The corollary is that the local bacteria are drug resistant, and you will need bigger doses than you would at home. Greek pharmacists, for instance, no longer sell any antibiotic (in pill form) of less than 500 mg.

Backache
Consider whether this is caused by tiredness, cold, or poorly designed seating, as if so the remedies are simple and obvious.

Baths *see* Aches and pains

Cold
Cold is not good for us. It stiffens the joints, slows the thought processes, and makes us more prone to chest infections and seasickness. Be wary, especially at night. Wear a few more garments than you think you might need if it is chilly, including a hat and scarf. You can always discard if you find you are too warm, but if you gradually become cold without noticing you might lose the impetus to go below for more clothes. See **Hypothermia**.

We should remind you that the winters in Europe, and even in the Mediterranean, are cold. So is Florida until you are well south. It follows that the boat needs heating. Our woodstove has been a godsend. We may be kippered when the wind is in the wrong direction, but we are warm and dry. This is not just a big boat solution; we have seen on a thirty foot boat a woodburning pot-belly stove which was dismantled and put in the forepeak for the summer.

A hot water bottle or two, with good thick cloth covers, are worth their space.

Damp
We are continually having to disabuse shorebased people who seem to think that living on the water means living in a perpetually damp atmosphere. It even led to a Turkish doctor insisting on treating Bill for rheumatism which he did not have: ('because he lived in a boat, which is damp,') instead of the slipped disc which was the actual cause of the trouble. A boat, if you think of it, is built to keep the water out, and is usually a lot drier than most houses. We say 'usually' because of course sometimes water gets in, mostly through condensation. This is a problem that should be thoroughly addressed by adequate ventilation to all cupboards, lockers, drawers and bilges, and minimisation of the cold surfaces that attract this unwelcome indoor dew, such as glass, steel and aluminium. It pays to keep your boat warm and airy, and have somewhere to put wet oilies till you can hang them out to dry. (The bath?...)

Diet

We do not eat as much as we did when young. This is normally fine when the choice of food is wide and varied, and the weather is good. On long passages when the sea is unkind, it is all too easy to say not only that we do not feel like cooking, but that we do not feel like eating either. We all know what we are supposed to include in a healthy diet, but sometimes we are too tired and it is too difficult to organise.

Make it less difficult. Have easily available in the galley some sustaining treats which will tempt you to eat. At times of stress your tooth will be sweeter than normal, and you will be thankful for chocolate bars, biscuits (Muesli biscuits or Granola bars make a good breakfast), fruit cake, boiled sweets, apples and oranges. Organise an easy way of making hot drinks. When the weather improves you can go back on to normal food.

Exercise

But, you will say, surely sailing is enough exercise already? Of course. It occasionally exercises you rather too much, even if you do not get caught in bad weather. The wind can die, and it's a long row home. Something can go wrong with the roller gear, leading to unwelcome overactivity of both our limbs and our adrenalin. If this happens, try and share the rough stuff, rest whenever you can, waste no energy on peripherals, and pace yourself with care. If we have had a day (or night) that has physically tired us, and conditions are now improved or at least on 'hold', we declare a Sunday, and take it very easy.

On the other hand resting all day in bed does not work for us. Spending too long in any position seizes the joints. Unless you are at anchor or the quayside for long periods this is unlikely to be your problem. Rocking chairs are known to be good for you, and what is a boat but an enormous rocking chair? Your muscles are continuously making small compensating movements as the boat moves. This is good for them, in moderation, taking sustenance to where it is needed and keeping everything well oiled. Sometimes the ankles, back and stomach muscles get overtired, and here a bucket seat and seat-belt might help.

We find that on normal days it pays to mix spells of standing with spells of sitting, and work spells with rest spells. If the work is hard, painting or engine-room work, it is best done early in the day, as then we have more energy and it is cooler.

While running a boat is good exercise for some parts of us, including the brain, remember the phrase 'Use it or lose it', and exercise the rest of you once a day, by putting each joint through its full range of motion. Start with a good stretch as the cat does, and be sure you are warm before you begin.

When at anchor and dinghying ashore, we row or sail. This keeps shoulders working and the tummy muscles from flabbing. We never take violent exercise, unless our lives are threatened, and probably not even then. Maintaining a boat seems to keep both boat and boaters in trim. Brisk walks are for the military, and hearty swimming for Olympic medallists unless you are in training for these things. Laurel walks gently to the market. (Bill is a good walker. Limited to her pace, he often complains that if he has to walk any slower he will lose his balance and fall over.) Climb slowly up to the castle. Swim and splash about, it reaches parts that sailing does not get to. Then have a siesta. Do not overdo *anything*.

Falls

Even young yachtspeople have falls, usually from leaping before they look. It is probably the most frequent cause of injury in yachting. Since we do ourselves more damage than the young do, and heal more slowly, we must take more care. Few things need to be done fast if you have chosen the right boat, and keep alert enough to see trouble before it happens. Falls occur:

- *In bad weather*, or disturbed conditions, do *sit down* as much as possible. This includes foredeck work. In a crisis Laurel is sometimes needed for this, instead of, as usual, steering. She does it sitting on the deck if she possibly can.
- *Getting in and out of the dinghy*, either on the quay or back at the boat. Use a bathing ladder, and head for the steps at the quayside if there are any. If not it is often easier to beach the dinghy and get your feet wet than trying to heave your reluctant body up a high stone quay.
- *Over-enthusiastic jumping ashore* with mooring lines is a pastime we should leave to the young. We must, however, learn to throw ropes a fair distance. We wish someone would invent a rope launcher that would shoot your mooring line accurately over a bollard. We suppose shooting it through one of those rings that grind your knuckles into the concrete is too much to expect.

See also under **Accidents**.

Feet

Since they are normally our only contact with the ground, feet need to be hardwearing. Thus any foot troubles must be promptly dealt with. Bad feet can sour your disposition; it is very rare to find someone with a benign expression and bad feet. Well-fitting shoes make happy feet and cheerful mariners. Bare feet are better than slippers in some respects, but put your shoes on before you do any boatwork. A stubbed bare toe at a critical moment can be the First Big Mishap leading to disaster. You can tell the real seamen: they do not man-oeuvre with bare feet.

Galley

The galley must be well planned, not tucked into an awkward space that no one else wants to use. It will be well ventilated (though the draught must not blow out the gas), preferably with an outlook for the cook that gives him/her a bit more to look at than someone's feet in ancient Docksiders or that seagull at the top of the mast. (This is not just a pleasant amenity, it helps the cook to avoid seasickness).

Permanent fiddles fitted to the stove to prevent accidents can make it more difficult to slide pans about, and this is a consideration with heavy items like pressure cookers which are so important in a boat. There are several kinds of fiddle that can be quickly put into place if you expect bad weather, and dispensed with when not needed. Stoves on gimbals make sense in a smallish boat, but we think are not so valuable in a larger one. A crash bar should be placed in front of the stove. Any hot pipes must be well lagged or insulated.

An easy galley will have drawers below waist level rather than cup-boards which can be hard to reach into. The drawer carcases will be built athwartships to minimise the chance of the drawers ending up on the floor. There will be a fridge. Why should we not have the comfort of cool drinks to refresh the Indian summer of our days, apart from the benefits of keeping perishables fresh and avoiding unwelcome bacilli and bluebottles.

Burns To minimise the risk of burns and scalds make sure that you have handy in the galley:

- A grabrail
- Somewhere safe to put down hot pans
- A good thick panholder or pair of oven gloves, renewed before hard use wears them too thin to be effective
- A fire blanket
- An aerosol spray for burns (if there is cold water in the washing up basin and the burn is minor, dip the burn in it at once; you will probably save it from blistering)
- A pressure cooker. (Even if the cooker falls off the stove, the lid will not fall off the cooker, as could happen with ordinary saucepans even with well-fitting lids. Once you have had soup or spaghetti all over your kitchen floor, or worse, over your pinny, you will see the force of the argument).

● If the manufacturers of your appliances have been thoughtless enough to label the knobs with instructions that are no use to you either because they are too small to read, or consist of elegant but ambiguous symbols that mean nothing to you at all, blow the designers a raspberry by making your own sticky labels with a felt pen, using clear arrows for 'off' and 'on' in nice big letters.

Bugs and bluebottles   Discourage flies. Anything they think delectable should be in the fridge, under a flyproof cover, or chucked overboard as soon as possible. Another plus for drawers is that they are easier to clean and debug than the usual awkward cupboard space, filled with unhealthy corners and crevices.

Glasses
Losing them is a hazard, either overboard, definitively, or down the back of the sofa, temporarily. If reading glasses is all you need, buy several pairs of the cheap reading spectacles available at Boots or a drug store, and hope that it is those that go overboard and not your expensive bifocals. If your sight needs correcting in other ways, be sure to take your prescription with you. We have had a good experience with faxing for a replacement with our credit card number. The glasses came quickly by post.

Have spectacle holders in many strategic places, particularly near the chart table. Plastic lenses are lighter and do not break, but they need care if they are not to get scratched. It could be a good idea to put a metal tag on the frame, so that they can be retrieved from the sea bottom with a magnet (If you do this, do not use them for taking bearings with a magnetic compass).

> Twinkle, twinkle, bunch of keys
> At the bottom of the seas
> Since you're ferrous where's the magnet?
> (Plastic objects need a dragnet)

Hospitals
In many places hospitals are as good or better than ours in England. A few words of explanation might be in order, however. In Greece and Italy the medical treatment in hospitals can be extremely good, but the surgeons surge and the nurses nurse, and the cleaners clean the wards. Nothing else. All other care of the patient is done by the family who camp round the bed, sometimes with portable cooking stoves, to feed and cherish their sick. Benighted yachtsmen with no friend or family to do this office have sometimes avoided starvation only by the cour-

tesy and kindness of the next bed's family sharing their food, or fetching him something from the taverna. The system is not worse than ours. Just different.

Hot weather
Not quite as bad for you, some say, as too much cold, but a recent heatwave in Athens with temperatures in the 40's (centigrade) carried off many elderly people. In hot climates good awnings, not too heavy and easily put up and taken down, are necessary. Consider a fixed awning over your steering position if you have no wheelhouse. At sea there is almost always a refreshing breeze, but in some harbours and canals the heat can be very uncomfortable, and a battery operated fan may contribute to your wellbeing.

Heat Stroke is the more lethal of the conditions caused by excessive heat and humidity, the other being *heat exhaustion*. Both give symptoms of headache, dizziness, and restlessness. With heat exhaustion, the victim will have sweated a great deal, and the skin will be cold and clammy. Put him in as cool a place as can be found, and restore fluids and salt, using 1/4 teaspoon of salt to a pint of water, or ready made Dioralyte. Recovery should be rapid. If sweating ceases, however, the patient's temperature rises, (it can go up to 40°C or 104°F) and he complains of feeling hot, rapid cooling is necessary before collapse ensues. Get medical help if available. Wrap the sufferer in a wet sheet and fan him with a newspaper if you have no electric fan. Bring the body temperature down to 38°C (98.4°F) and repeat the procedure if necessary.

HRT or Hormone Replacement Therapy
There seems to be less controversy over this now than there used to be. Female mariners should discuss with their doctor whether they might benefit, given that half of all post-menopausal women suffer from osteoporosis (thinning of the bones) and that the risk of fractures is perhaps higher in a boat than at home on land. If the answer is yes, you will be advised to have a six monthly check-up.

Hypothermia
This kills more often than drowning, and is the more to be feared because its approach is insidious. Take cold weather very seriously, keep warm and dry, or failing that warm and wet. Wet wool is warmer than wet cotton or nylon. Windproof clothing must be worn outside the wool, as the wind can chill very fast, faster still if you are wet. Since 20% of heat is lost through the head, be sure to cover it.

Signs of hypothermia are:

- The body temperature sinks to below 35°C (94°F)
- Movement slows
- The brain slows
- Breathing becomes slow and shallow
- Speech slows and becomes huskier
- There is no complaint of feeling cold
- Drowsiness begins
- Normally warm areas of the body (armpits etc) feel cold to the touch

If the victim can still move enough to get into it, a warm (not hot) bath can be given, and warm (but not hot) drinks administered. If they cannot move, do not bathe. Rewarming someone elderly who is almost unconscious must be done very gently indeed, so as not to strain the heart, and is best achieved by putting the sufferer in a warm (25°C, 75°F) atmosphere and preventing further heat loss by wrapping him in reflective space blankets, covering the head, nose, and mouth with a scarf.

It follows that your medical kit should include:

- A rectal thermometer for low body temperatures (the ordinary mouth thermometer will not do)
- Space blankets (made of reflective foil, they take up very little room)
- A thermometer to measure cabin temperature

Legionnaire's disease

Water tanks, lying stagnant for several months over the winter, are a perfect breeding-ground for various bacteria. The first flotilla and bareboat customers in spring probably will not drink from these tanks, but they may well shower from them, and some of the bacteria which are typically nurtured in these conditions love being distributed in a spray. The nastiest of these bugs is *Legionella*, and older folk are especially vulnerable to it.

We have often observed that elderly yachtspeople early in each season are prone to chest infections. We came across several cases around Easter time last year. No diagnoses were made, the causes were not investigated, and the sufferers appeared to recover quite well.

The possibility of *Legionella* multiplying in the tanks of laid-up boats is well known in principle, but was completely unknown to the boatyard workers to whom we talked. Be aware of the problem, and remember that it can affect the private owner, too. We give some guidance on prevention, and would welcome some reassurance from charter companies that they are aware of the problem, and take steps to flush the water systems of their yachts thoroughly at the start of the season.

An excellent article by Ian Brown in *The Little Ship* (the Journal of the Little Ship Club) describes the risks of infection in small boats by Legionnaire's disease (which causes initial symptoms like a bad attack of 'flu). It is a risk for the following reasons.

● It attacks the older age group, especially if you already suffer from chest infections.
● The fresh water system in boats promotes the growth of the bacteria due to stagnation, high temperatures, and extensive use of plastic materials.
● The bacteria are spread by droplets in a confined space, such as obtains in the shower compartment.

You are particularly at risk if you are male, 40 to 70 years old, a smoker, drinker, or with chronic respiratory disease.

The risk is especially great when stagnant water lies in plastic tubing and tanks for long periods at high temperatures, so if you live on board permanently the conditions which favour it are less likely.

If you leave your boat over winter, or for several months, Eur. Ing. Brown suggests that the water services should be disinfected before use or at least twice a year, ensuring that all parts of the system are treated thoroughly as follows:

1   First drain down the entire system.
2   Refill the storage tanks with water chlorinated at a rate of 20-50 mg/litre (20-50 ppm).
3   Allow the chlorinated water to flow to all parts of the system by successively opening the outlets such as taps and showers until there is a smell of chlorine.
4   Close the outlets and allow the system to stand for an appropriate period. This period depends on the chlorine concentration, varying from at least an hour at 50 ppm to at least two hours at 20 ppm. *DON'T FORGET TO WARN THE CREW* that chlorination is in progress.
5   After disinfection is complete, the system should be flushed through thoroughly with fresh water.

Chlorinating agents such as Milton 2 Sterilizing fluid are easily obtained from chemists, and supermarkets, often in the Baby Care section. Precautions in use should be strictly observed.

Rest
Siestas are one of the pleasures of retirement. Be sure not to intersperse your little plan-making sessions with violent activity, and you

will live long. Incidentally it is very important to impose a siesta on your guests, whatever their ages, or yours will be seriously disturbed. They may do what they like, as long as it is quiet and does not involve you. Everyone benefits, as you all meet again at teatime with sunny tempers and plenty to talk about.

Seasickness

> Rockaby lady, tucked in your bunk,
> Let's hope it's only cocoa you've drunk.
> When the storm breaks you could feel quite ill
> Make sure you've taken your seasickness pill.

Whatever your age, seasickness is a misery. Find the pill that suits you best and take it in plenty of time. Do not mix with alcohol. If your teeth are not home grown, take them out before you lose them overboard with your breakfast.

If you are on daily medication for some condition, ask your doctor's advice about whether to replace the pills you vomit. Crackers and Bovril can usually be swallowed if seasickness has got you, but a plate of porridge *before* you are seasick works even better.

Skin

Like an old mackintosh, our skin loses its plasticity with age. Since you will be abusing it with strong sun, wind and salt water you should take a little more care of it when you can. At best it will roughen, dry and flake, especially on the shins and elbows; at worst it can crack, infect, and develop ulcers that are hard to heal. Male mariners may rejoice to hear that there is some truth in the words of the old song: 'Too much washin'll weaken yer', (they always knew it was a waste of precious water), but it is too much soap and bath salts that dry the skin, and both male and female mariners will benefit after a shower from massaging with something to keep in the moisture, like after-sun moisturizer, cocoa butter, or even simple baby oil.

Teeth

These, if not firmly attached to you, can easily join your glasses in the briny. Even if they are stainless steel, the magnet will not get them back. Always take them out if you feel seasick, and try and remember where you put them. If you no longer grow your own teeth, take a spare pair of dentures, and ask your dentist for a repair kit in case of breakage.

It goes without saying that a dental checkup before you go should be on your departure list.

Vitamin tablets

Ideally, you should not need these. If your diet has been restricted on a long passage, or because of bad weather, a few Multivitamin capsules might be useful, especially if you are single-handed and your resistance to infection seems low. Get back on to good food as soon as you can.

Weightlifting

> Jack and Jill are over the hill
> And can't carry pails of water.
> It's far more jolly to purchase a trolley
> Than ask for help from your daughter.

When, in our youth, we bought the old cruising boat *Barracuda*, built in 1896, we kept her at the Yarmouth yard of the East Anglian Cruising Club. This was a do-it-yourself co-operative yard and during hauling out and launching times everyone was expected to be there at weekends to lend a hand.

When a launch was imminent, all the middle-aged would go and shuffle at the back of a woodpile, or look very busy with a varnish brush, since they all had bad backs. Most of the younger ones were busy acquiring them, with enthusiastic 'Hup!'s and 'Heave Ho!'s, and more vocal enthusiasm than physical skill. It was the older men who, moving slowly and deliberately, never pushing or straining, knew how to move five tons of awkwardness (a boat out of the water is an ungainly thing) from here to there without busting a gut in either human or boat.

'Give me a place to stand and a long enough lever and I could move the earth'. So said Archimedes. When Bill was young during the war he went to help out in his uncle's boatyard, building small craft for the Admiralty. One of the shipwrights had returned to work to do his bit for the common cause ('I knew you 'ouldn't be able to git on without me'). He was 91, and a mastmaker by trade (you should have seen his tools; axes of all shapes and sizes, and all razor sharp). He mostly did odd jobs because his eyesight was not so good, and one of his tasks was to move boats that had been hauled out for repair round the yard.

For this purpose he would generally use a crabwinch leading the wires through various dead eyes in the ground, but if the move was a small one or was a lift, he used levers. He worked mostly on his own, occasionally with young Bill as his mate. By himself he could raise a ten-ton boat a couple of feet in the air and chock her up. He took his time but he got there doing it by judiciously placed levers, an inch at a time, first at this end, then at that.

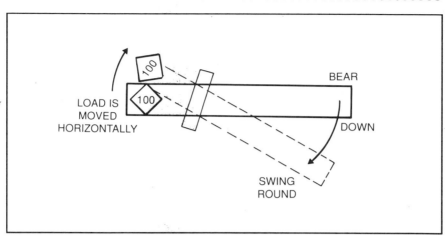

Fig 1

He could move a boat sideways with levers, not necessarily as one so often sees by a vertical lever shoving something over on greased ways, but by lifting and then swinging the lever before setting down once more. (See Fig 1.)

He was a tiny little man, and his prowess made a lasting impression on Bill. There is no need, he maintains, for people in boats to have bad backs in spite of all the heavy weights that need moving round. All that is required is an understanding of levers, of rollers, and of the use of tackles, which seamen, just to be different, pronounce tay-ckles.

Some people like to add small winches to this list, but Bill believes the circular motion of the handle while under strain puts the back at risk. It is all very well pulling or pushing the handle at the top or bottom of the circle, (we are speaking of a horizontal drum) but the change from pulling to lifting or bearing down is a danger point. Every round turn of the handle has two such danger points. Winding horizontally one has less power.

Tackles, too, can give problems if the hauling parts are not handled correctly. A good tug-of-war crew knows the secret: anchor your feet with legs bent and arms and back straight. Then straighten your legs; the tension you can safely exert this way is enormous with little chance of self damage. The secret, therefore, is to see that the hauling part passes through a leading block so that you pull horizontally in a good direction.

One of the problems with using a tackle such as a handy billy, is finding a suitable hook directly over the load. Fig 2 shows how two tackles can be used to make a good lift. You do not have to work both tackles at the same time, it is perfectly all right to adjust each a bit at a

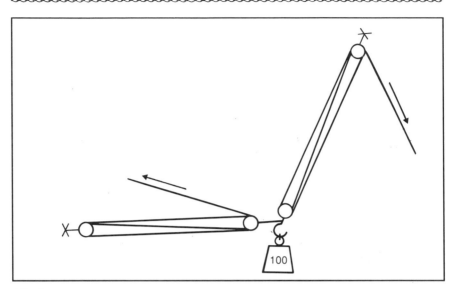

Fig 2

time. It takes longer: are you in a hurry? Well, you should have started earlier.

Fig 3 shows how levers can be used repeatedly to raise loads by quite large amounts, and also to swing them. How did old Billy the shipwright lift five tons? He would have needed a long lever. He set up his lever safely with one end under the boat, and then on the other end he placed 28 lb weights one at a time until he had enough to balance the boat which might, with a ten to one ratio, need forty weights. He would achieve his final delicate balance by moving the final weight horizontally along the lever, and then take his time chocking her up.

If he wanted to raise a boat only an inch or so, he would use wedges, which he would place at intervals along her chocks. Wedges can lift enormous loads. At launching of big ships, the whole enormous weight used to be lifted off her building chocks on to the launching ways by hundreds of wedges, all being struck simultaneously by shipwrights in time with the master's whistle. It is fascinating watching 10,000 tons being lifted in this way.

The lesson for moving heavy weights is to plan every move so that your body comes under no unfair strain, then do it at a pace that is under your command. If you have to lower the weight, then it is equally important that there is no possibility of the weight taking charge. Make every movement a controlled one.

Most of us know that if you *must* lift, it should be done with the back straight, using the legs, which are the strongest weight bearers in

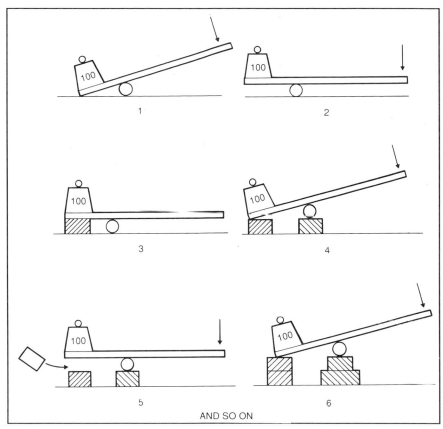

Fig 3. How old Billy the Shipwright used levers to move very heavy weights easily.

the body. If you want to move something heavy sideways, put your back to it and push with the legs.

One weight-lifting chore is provisioning the boat if you are cruising. You do not shop as often as you do when living ashore and all that stuff has to be carried aboard, and often quite a distance from the market. A shopping trolley is essential if you are not to make too many trips. It has other uses as well. But try to find a trolley which (a) does not rust, and (b) folds, preferably with removable wheels, for these always stick out awkwardly.

While we are on weightlifting, here is another 'I'm glad I'm not young any more' story.

A singlehander moored his yacht at the side of the Canal du Midi, and went ashore to buy eggs from an old couple at a nearby farmhouse. Late at night there was a rapping on his hull: Could Monsieur help them as he was young and strong, and there was a weight to be carried? At this time of night? Well, yes, he could. Back at the farmhouse, they took him upstairs. It is the old mother, they said, would he lift the extremely old lady there in bed down to the pickup truck in the yard, and stay with them to do the reverse at the other end of the journey? He soon realised that he had no need to apologise to his burden for manhandling her, since she was dead. He carried the body down as requested, and stayed with it while they drove about ten kilometres to a cottage where other ancient relatives awaited, carried the old lady up to bed, where they laid her reverently down and arranged her nicely with hands crossed, quick, before she stiffened. Then he asked them why. It was simple, they explained. She was visiting one of her sons at the farmhouse when she died. They had brought her back to her own house here, across the border in another département. For bureaucratic reasons, she must die here, for if she died in a different département, the young monsieur would understand, the paperwork ensuing, the trouble with the héritage, and worst of all, the *expense!* All would now be well, maintenant one telephones the docteur. A thousand thanks, Monsieur, a dozen new-laid eggs tomorrow morning, perhaps?

14

Remembering Not to Forget

It's hard to remember
Which club you're a member
And even the name of your yacht?
Hang on to your reason that's playing you treason,
Try not to forget you forgot.

WE HAVE ALWAYS LIKED the charming explanation of an elderly man who had forgotten our names: 'I'm so sorry,' he said 'the brain cell with your names on it just died'. More devious was the ploy of another aged and forgetful friend: 'Now, what outfit are you with, again?'

Now that our own brain cells are dying with fair rapidity, or their contents getting wiped, we are having to evolve many stratagems in order to remember essential details.

Lists

What are the essential details that we must remember? Things that head the list involve the seaworthiness and safety of your boat, and the safety and welfare of its crew. Almost anything else can cheerfully be forgotten. Make your own list, since one does not want to encumber the memory with needless data. Whether you like it or not, your memory will perversely keep in mind a library-full of interesting and little known facts about pyrography or the properties of selenium, while allowing you to forget a sunsight or the weather forecast.

It helps to make lists, but do not lose them. They are a major weapon in the memory war. An ongoing notebook, strongly bound, is Bill's talisman, he finds things in it by date: this happened before that, so it will be: ah! here it is, after the BOAT SHOW, but before the NEW ENGINE. On the first page is his name and current forwarding address. As the book is small, he often forgets it in phone boxes, or leaves it on somebody's desk. Short of chaining it to his wrist, we have no answer to that yet. Lists and notes have to be made, and losing them is an almost insoluble problem. Few boats have space for a pin board where it is not subject to a gale of wind if you open a porthole or companionway. Notebooks are better than scraps of paper, anyway, and one big notebook is better than many easily mislaid smaller ones, a notebook large enough to be unlosable is perhaps the optimum.

We once thought that a boxfile came into this category, so we unearthed an old one, relabelled it MANUALS, and put in it all the irreplaceable stuff for engines, generator, autopilot, and so on. By the time we next needed one of the manuals, we'd lost the boxfile. After twenty-four hours of bitter recriminations and frantic search, one of us had a flash of inspiration. The boxfile sat on the shelf exactly where it should have been, but the new label had come off, and the one underneath read, as formerly, COOKING HINTS.

It comes hard to a couple of slobs like us, but constantly losing things is forcing us into tidier habits. If a thing is not in its proper place it is *lost*. If it is not adequately labelled, it is just as lost.

We buy different coloured notebooks if possible, so that Bill's notes are on blue and Laurel's notes on pink. This idea is capable of further extension as you can get notebooks with green and yellow paper too. Whatever the colour, the sheets tend to wander if detached.

Lists of stores, edible or not, lists of work to be done and maintenance to be kept up, help you to keep track.

We also keep a paint book. Not outline drawings to crayon in, but a record of what got painted when, and what with, and how much we used, together with the 'recipe' or instructions for some glazes and two-part paints and their solvents. This is valuable because the inevitable spill on the outside of the paint tin always obliterates the most vital instructions. These modern paints are so chemically lethal that the instructions read like those for throwing a hand grenade: 'Take out the pin and count to –' and that's the bit that's unreadable under the paint splodge, when you've already taken out the pin.

Decide if the thing to be remembered is time-related like sunsights, or event-related like dropping the anchor, or neither, like cleaning and maintenance. A fourth category includes things to be remembered in an emergency; here lists are a help but not the complete answer. Different strategies help with different categories, but one strategy tops them all:

Routine
This is one of the most effective overall stratagems. If a thing becomes part of your routine, it is quite hard to forget it. We have no difficulty in remembering to have breakfast, or to get dressed. Not yet, anyway. Many very old people retain a moderately firm grip on their lives only

by this means. The clock and the calendar are paramount, which can be exasperating for their kin, but it works for them: eleven o'clock is coffee time, Sunday morning is Church, and Monday is clean clothes and washday.

Time-based routine

Takes in such things as sunsights and the weather forecasts which occur at specific times. Unlike these, maintenance and cleaning are hard to relate to anything specific, they are not time-sensitive like taking sunsights, or event-sensitive like What to Do before Anchoring. It makes sense, therefore, to give them a time-slot: (every Tuesday), or an event slot: (the imminent arrival of visitors).

Note that a daily or weekly routine is easier to maintain, because oftener and more ingrained in the mind, than a monthly or yearly one, hence the ease of remembering breakfast. The time slot is probably preferable for cleaning and maintenance, as there is enough to do before the arrival of visitors without extra event-related items.

We know this leads to little obsessions like washing the galley floor every Monday morning (unless the ship is actually sinking,) and cleaning the seacocks every Feast of Saints Simon and Jude, but may we be forgiven, the floor *does* get washed and the seacocks *do* get cleaned.

Engine routines are very difficult to slot in as they depend on hours run. This is almost impossible to monitor without machines known as hour-meters which read off the total time to date that the engine has been running. It is advisable to have such machines, and then to remember to look at them. Their dials should be alongside the engine rev counter, at which one does actually have to look from time to time. Alternatively, keep a tally of hours run in the log.

Items which depend on short-term time are things like cooking the stew in the pressure cooker, and that suggests an excellent memory aid for all these time slots: using a kitchen timer, preferably a four-hour one which helps with changing watches at sea. Modern radios can often be set to come on in time for the forecast, but you must remember to be there to hear it. Sometimes there is a lot of background noise at sea, especially in conditions where the weather forecast becomes important, and a loud alarm can help. An alarm watch has its uses as a reminder of when to go and listen to a forecast, or take your sight, but the buttons are very fiddly for stiff fingers. The sort of kitchen timer that hangs round your neck is a lot easier to manage, though it is heavier than a knot in your handkerchief.

Things that should be remembered at rather vague intervals are best given a time or date slot. These can be noted down in a notebook, or a card index, or in the ship's log, and can be ticked off with a dated signature and great satisfaction.

While we are on lists, the ship's log should help you to remember many things: you need a page-a-day diary, and a checklist at the back. Then you will notice if you have not jotted down the engine hours, or that you topped up with water, or that the gas bottle ran out yesterday and therefore will again in X weeks' time.

Event-based routine

Here cultivating good habits, even parrot fashion, helps you to remember everything that goes with a particular event. Generations of sailors have learnt the rule of the road by rote; Bill remembers one senior Captain RN who could occasionally be heard muttering on the bridge:

> If to your starboard Red appear
> It is your duty to keep clear...

and:

> Green to Green and Red to Red
> Perfect safety, go ahead...

which brings us nicely to:

Mnemonics

These rhymes and phrases to aid the memory can help with many events; take anchoring, for example. Bill finds the right spot, Laurel does almost everything else unless assistance is required. She looks at the anchor winch and thinks:

Brake on?
Ratchet out?
Clutch out? Then:
Slip (ie let go when ready)

You will notice that the initials are those of the British Red Cross Society, and this mnemonic helps her to remember these checks. She sometimes forgets to hoist the black ball after anchoring, as it is difficult to add another B to her mnemonic, or an A for anchor light at night.

Bill keeps on murmuring Billy Went Yachting Round Bethnal Green, and wondering why he remembers it, without remembering what it means. He thinks it was something to do with collision mats in First World War battleships which is the sort of important thing he was examined in at Naval College in 1945. He also barks out FUCLAPS now and then in a voice heavy with the Power of Command. It makes an inoffensive swearword, but he is also trying to remember what it means by taking it by surprise. So far his only recall is that in this special case FU stands for Funnel Upright. He has concluded that it lacks present day significance, and is trying, unsuccessfully, to stop thinking about it.

We have made the anchor light easier to remember by associating it with switching off the Nav. lights, part of the post-voyage:

Cockpit check

This is another aid to memory, which becomes second nature after a while, though it needs lists until it is burned into the brain. Most professionals have printed cockpit check-lists on a clip board and go through the items one by one, crossing them off in sequence even if they know the whole thing by heart. This is the way to avoid mistakes, and it is comforting to know that it is common in aircraft cockpits. The pre-voyage cockpit check prevents you from leaving harbour without the cat or the captain. We have twice in sixteen years had to go back for the cat, once three-quarters of an hour back up the canal at Missolonghi, where we found our Nelson having a second breakfast on a nearby freighter, and once three hours back to Hydra where she was asleep on a fishing boat. The harbour was by this time too full to get into and the cat, annoyed and prickly, was passed with the alacrity of politicians getting rid of a parcel bomb across several boats to her welcoming family. The captain has been left behind only once, having leapt ashore with a rope that was not made fast inboard, leaving Laurel alone on *Fare Well* with a strong cross wind. Desperation improved her berthing competence mightily, and she got him back. Of course this contretemps was due to sheer incompetence, not failure of memory.

The post-voyage check assists you to sleep well, knowing that all is safe and switched off. Except the anchor light.

Place-related memory

This seems, like photographic memory, to be a gift. Bill has it. He can draw the plan of a harbour he has entered only once, and that twenty years ago, and tell you just where the post office is. Laurel can tell you who we met and what we did, but cannot find the post office. In case the gift lets us down, we collect town plans, usually freely available from the tourist bureaux, and keep them by countries and then alphabetically in a box file. We also have a tin full of cards and postcards of hotels and restaurants that we have particularly liked. Occasionally we mislay the tin.

People-related memory

Most long term yotties have a visitor's book, in which to record the boats and people they meet on the way. We recently met someone whose memory was badly affected by a head injury, who takes a polaroid photo of all visitors so as not to forget them, an excellent extension to the concept.

Emergency-related memory

You can make lists till the cows come home, but there is no remedy here but instinctive reaction, like putting on the brakes when you see tail-lights close ahead. You can do this in a car because you have done it so often. You must become just as familiar with danger looming on a boat.

Fast reactions can limit the damage if not avoid it altogether, and since we are not as fast as we were, we must start earlier, ie notice the problem quickly. Situations requiring fast action should be rehearsed until they become old friends, a routine, in fact. Some dangers afloat tend to come at you slower because of the slower speed you travel at, but your avoiding action takes longer to happen too; you cannot just put the brake on and stop.

Recent studies on memory and learning show that most of us can hold seven items of information in our minds at once in our short term memory. This number is increased if the item is processed in a different part of the brain, ie speech is different from listening is different from visual stimulus. Which explains why the captain can hold a great deal in the forefront of his mind in an emergency, and still be able to swear at you when you bring him further bad news. Seriously, it is probably a good idea if your emergency lists are fairly brief, and that you read them aloud sometimes to stimulate the listening part of your brain. Nothing, in the end, can take the place of experience, but to be prepared is half the battle, and you will learn extremely fast while something untoward is happening. Go over these events with your companions afterwards, several times, to make sure that what you have learnt becomes experience, and goes into your long term memory.

Stowage and storage for the forgetful

You need to know:

> What you've got
> Where you've put it
> How much you have left, which leads to
> What you need to shop for.

This means the notebook again, backed up by lists. We find that it is a good idea to put a list of the contents of a locker inside a plastic sandwich bag and tape the bag to the lid as flat as possible, it is less likely to be torn or dislodged by rummaging hands. If you use squared paper it is easy to block in so many tins of Y with //// and then cross them off as you use them, XXX.

We also try to keep a Where is it? notebook that covers every item on board, with a plan of all cupboards, lockers and stowage spaces. The trouble here is nomenclature. One of us might want to find a heater which the other has filed under 'stove'. Copious cross references are necessary, and this can lead to trouble after up-dating or other alteration.

Lockers

> Old Mother Docker
> Went to a locker,
> Looking for something for supper.
> What wasn't too old
> Had beetles or mould;
> She'd forgotten to stow it in Tupper.

Lockers in many boats tend to be uncomfortably deep, and benefit from dividing up with bins, square flower pot holders, buckets and so on. To sort your tins into plastic bags is a last resort. Unless they are very strong the bags chafe, split and tear, and pieces will end up blocking the bilge pump, to the wrath of the skipper, and danger to the ship.

Cardboard packets do not survive longer than a weekend cruise, so you need to transfer the contents into something more durable, with a wellfitting lid. There are many useful plastics containers on the market now, but do not spurn the lowly coffee jar, which has cheapness and durability to recommend it. Cut a cardboard label from the packet with any instructions and the use-by date, and transfer it to the jar. The ubiquitous presence of weevils when in warmer climes is another strong recommendation for glass, or heavy plastic containers (they chomp through thin plastic).

As our eyesight is not what it might be, given that we have our head in a dark locker as often as not, large labels are sometimes useful; use a waterproof felt pen and the colour coded labels as used in freezers to get your stores really well signposted; but do not rely on reputedly sticky labels actually sticking for long, add a strip of sellotape right round the container, otherwise you might end up as we did after a hot summer, with lots of nude jars containing substances that looked like flour but weren't, and a heap of curly dried up labels at the bottom of the drawer. We have mentioned, have we not, that drawers are easier to cope with than lockers if you can manage it. You probably cannot avoid lockers altogether, but make sure that the lids are not too big and heavy to lift, are hinged rather than loose, and have some method of holding them up while you rummage, otherwise they land with a thwack on your head or hands.

Belgian boats, we are told, carry a special slatted locker for potatoes, just as our Dutch barge did. (It was under the skipper and wife's box bed.) Fresh produce ought to be somewhere easy to see and pick over, otherwise a decaying cabbage could get forgotten and cause a nasty surprise next spring. Nothing is worse (well, almost nothing) than feeling in a locker for a potato and finding something soggy, so the slats for ventilation make sense. Nets seem to be the popular solution for fruit. Why not build in a vegetable basket? If you can get it out to clean under it sometimes so much the better, you avoid an accumulation of onion skins and withered knobs which might once have been courgettes.

Bottles and jars

These come in all shapes and sizes, and are best left that way as memory is helped by familiar shapes and colours. We all know the Worcester sauce and the Gordon's gin without having to read the label. Big bottles stow into holes cut for them, smaller ones fit on a narrow shelf with an adequate preventer in front of them. If some of the bottles are plastic, intersperse them with the glass ones as buffers to reduce both chink and breakages.

Dycem

This is a nonslip plastic sheet that can be cut to fit anywhere it might be needed, under the bottles on their shelf for example, or a circle under the fruit bowl. It is expensive if bought as fancy place mats at the chandlers, but is available by the metre. Its properties are temporarily lost if it is dusty, greasy, or wet, so it needs an occasional clean. Fiddles round the table can almost be dispensed with except in very heavy weather, as the dinner will fall off your plate before the plate slides off the plastic. A bulkier non-slip alternative is a damp sponge-cloth. This is useful on the draining board to prevent the pots sliding. A wire drainage rack firmly fixed on the draining board can help to keep a few items under control while you wash up. Another sponge cloth at the bottom of the sink bowl prevents breakages.

Spices and herbs

If you have no room for the neat little row of pots and bottles that everyone has in their kitchen these days (but fewer in their boats, though it's coming), furnish yourself with a number of resealable plastic bags about three inches by five (they can be had from jewellers and watchmakers' suppliers) and put your herbs and spices in these. Label carefully (with date) and keep them in a box with an airtight lid.

Dates and lists

You will find it useful to put dates or use-by information on almost everything. It tells you how much you use in a certain period, and what to replace before you run out. It aids you to make a list of what the next visitor might usefully bring with them from home, particularly things that go off in taste like creamed horseradish and tartare sauce, and cake mix, and things that are hard to find in foreign waters, like poppadums and Marmite.

Most of our coffee jars have been relabelled with instructions for the use of their contents, whatever they happen to be, even if it is as simple as 'One tbsp to $1/4$ pt water'. Some of our coffee jars actually have coffee in them.

It is numbers and quantities that we are most aware of forgetting these days, so another little notebook in a drawer in the galley has quantities for standard recipes: bread, pastry, Yorkshire pudding, egg custard, and so on.

15

Navigation for Short Memories

Sing a song of sextants, let Grannie have a try,
Four and twenty cosines multiplied by pi:
When the sum is added up, what is our position?
Somewhere in the carpark behind the Seaman's Mission.

IT MIGHT SEEM at first sight that navigation for older crews would be the same as for anyone else; merely a matter of getting safely from A to B. Well, not entirely. We have to cope with our ageing brain cells. We tire more easily. We tend to absent-mindedness, if not downright temporary amnesia.

A few years ago Bill read in the *Yachting Monthly* an excellent article by a fellow professional which in a few words pointed up one of the potential problems for the ageing navigator, though the writer, Richard Hutson, did not elaborate on this aspect. This is that navigation is taught as a position-finding craft, and that almost all emphasis is on knowing where you are, rather than where you are going. As one ages it gets more difficult to keep in mind several concepts at the same time. Mr Hutson points out that more vessels are wrecked knowing where they are, than when they do not. When you are lost you are careful. But when you get a good navigational fix it is too easy to note it down and then absent-mindedly amble off to brew some tea, forgetting that that is not the end of the matter. Absent-mindedness is a besetting problem.

So cultivate the habit of thinking ahead. The beautiful fix is history. It is past; you were safe then: now concentrate on the future. With Bill this has become habit, but Laurel likes to draw a 'one-hour circle' round a fix so she can make a positive check on any imminent danger. In fact, by doing this she also checks further ahead than one hour, so that it is a good discipline.

Landfalls

One of the most stressful (but exhilarating) things about navigating is making landfalls after a voyage out of sight of land for any reason (it could be bad visibility as well as distance), when you are not sure of your exact position.

This can also be the most dangerous part of the voyage, for the conditions that would throw doubt on your position would also be likely to increase your tiredness. Tired people are apt to be careless, too easily lulled into accepting the easiest or most convenient answer.

Jim and Ann Griffin, who had lived in a boat for forty years, lost *Northern Light* in this way after an Atlantic crossing. Tired out and in mediocre weather conditions they mistook the lighthouse they actually saw for the one with closely similar characteristics that they wanted to see, and were stranded off the coast of Spain. However good a navigator you are, no one is immune to weariness and loss of concentration. Bill has decided that he wants no more of such worries if he can avoid them and has bitten the Electronic Bullet. He has swallowed another Milliamp Pill, together with several other metaphors, always excepting swallowing the anchor. His faithful sextant is brought out more to be oiled and caressed than to be used nowadays. (At the rate he is going about reducing the stress factors in our boat he will soon spend most of the time napping in his chair, known on board as 'Passage planning').

So let us swallow our youthful prejudices and look at some electronic equipment.

Navigational machinery

As we have said, Bill has overcome his deep distrust and increased the amount of electronic equipment on board. Whereas we started our full-time cruising life in 1976 with minimum electronics, namely an echo-sounder to which was added a radar since it was a tool of Bill's trade (it was very seldom used). We very soon added an autopilot, finding it essential for short-handed, long distance cruising.

Then we went into a long period of resistance to any more newfangled ideas; based fairly soundly on many miles of cruising under many different conditions (and quite a bit of it without an engine either). Finally and recently, we made the last great concession, and aquired a GPS (global positioning system) navigator, and a NASA Navtex. The reasons for this capitulation are:

- Increase in age and decrease in energy
- The miniaturisation of much equipment
- The improvement in reliability
- A marked lowering of prices.

Echo sounder

This takes soundings continuously, and is of particular help with coastal navigation, as knowledge of the depth narrows down the spot on the chart where you might be, and even more important, tells you where you cannot be. The story goes of the crew who was told to call the skipper when he found five fathoms. The skipper was roused with the words, 'I haven't been able to find five fathoms, Skip. Will three do?'

No more of that with modern electronics, the salesmen claim; nowadays the sets have an alarm which can be set to call you at any given depth. Mostly, however, it calls you when you do not want to be called, because it has found a shoal of fish, or you have absent-mindedly forgotten to switch off the alarm. So, paradoxically, the alarm becomes a nuisance, a false friend, which discourages its use. If we left it switched on, we would be up every ten minutes to check on it, worse, it would become mere background noise. An alarm must be a palpable alarm. We find that the dial indicating eight feet under us is quite heart-stopping enough without bleeping noises as well. Repeated monitoring of instruments helps keep one alert.

Radar

In fog this is valuable for pilotage close to land. Salesmen make much of its potential for collision avoidance, but in a sailing yacht in the big ship lanes, this usually comes down to knowing by how little you have just been missed. That can be very unnerving. (It is more comfortable in any visibility to be out of the shipping lanes, but occasionally one has to cross them.) For collision avoidance, radar needs some training in order to make the best of it.

It is a helpful cross reference to check on other equipment, since it will tell you how far off the coastline is, and in what direction. If this does not square with what the echo sounder and the GPS are telling you, check the source information of your chart.

There are snags in using two methods of position fixing that are based on different concepts. Radar is a relative position indicator: it will give you your actual distance from a piece of land. GPS is a geographical indicator: it reads off your latitude and longitude. If your chart is an old one based on a horizontal datum that could not be reconciled with others, then simultaneous fixes taken with radar and GPS will appear in different places on the chart and present you, in poor visibility, with a choice of two courses to steer, one of which will be false. The Hydrographer is gradually replacing the centuries-old charts that can still be found among the 6000 or so that he publishes, but it will take time. For those of us off to distant parts where there may not be much commercial or military demand for the charts to be updated, it might take years, and we should all be careful to check the geographical basis of our charts when using electronics close to land. Our GPS recently perched us on top of a 500 metre high mountain, or so it seemed, like the Ark on Ararat. The longitude and latitude of the chart were together 1.2 miles out of place.

Autopilot

This takes a great load off the crew, and allows them to do other essential things like visit the heads, make cocoa, keep a look-out, or even check the navigation. An autopilot of some sort is now considered virtually essential for practically any sailor. Steering all the time by tiller or wheel can be a tyranny and can prevent you having sufficient personal resources to cope with mishaps. The problem is that autopilots get more and more complex; most now have a 'learning' microprocessor and quite frankly do more than we really want them to. The manufacturers say this does not add significantly to the cost; it is all software, they say. That may be so, but the trouble is that the little beasts are slow learners, not to say in the remedial class, and cannot anticipate. If you sheet in a sail and alter the balance, you, as a person, may be able to anticipate the change and adjust the trim on the autopilot, but you cannot do it if the manufacturer has not included a convenient knob to do it with.

All manufacturers of all electronic equipment should give a little more attention to waterproofing their hardware. Milliamps and moisture soon start fighting each other and moisture always wins. The slightest airleak allows damp salt air to be sucked in as the fitting cools and the air inside contracts, the water vapour in the air condenses, depositing its salt evenly on everything. When the temperature rises again the expanding air is expelled, leaving behind its salt crystals. Modern printed circuits rely on the tiniest traces of conductor which even one salt crystal can soon corrode. Only encapsulated circuits are reliably free from this potential problem.

Autopilots sometimes have irritating personal habits. Ours used to quail just before an Atlantic crossing, like a mistreated spouse saying 'I quit'. If it consented to work at all it could suddenly take you round in a perfect circle in mid-Atlantic.

All autopilots go into sulks if the waves get too much for them. Just when you need them most, you find you have to steer by hand. We know some experienced senior navigators who have two separate autopilots. We have not done that, but we understand why.

It is more than ever a good idea to avoid rough weather as we grow older. We will not entirely succeed, of course, and must be ready and able to cope with it when it comes, but to help with forecasting you might like to consider:

Saint Brendan the Navigator was over 80 when he set out from Galway with 17 fellow monks on the journey described in the 10th century manuscript: Brendan's Voyage. *Some say the Land of Promise he found was the Canaries, some say Iceland. The voyage lasted 8 years.*

Weatherfax
The Weatherfax receives and prints out synoptic charts of weather systems, and has improved a great deal since the days when proud owners, hypnotised by the sheer magic of it, would show us indecipherable smudges of grey on grey: ('Is that a front coming over, do you think? or a crease in the paper? Nasty storm down there. Oh, no, it's a thumb print.') It is now possible to get radio equipment which will print out personal fax as well as weather information. These machines are only as good as long-range radio propagation conditions, and you cannot always rely on good reception.

Navtex
Navigational warnings and weather forecasts are received by Navtex and stored in a memory. According to which model you have, it will then print out, or show the information on a mini TV screen. It does not yet cover the whole world, but is invaluable in North America and European waters. The TV version is not expensive.

GPS (Global Positioning System)
GPS is a little receiver/computer which buttons on to three or more satellites and works out your position from them. You need to know when it's lying, and though it is supposed to tell you when it is having difficulty, the error indicators in most sets are on a different 'page' to the one you are using.

It has to be borne in mind that GPS is an American military system that civilians are allowed to tune in to without charge. In order that potential enemies may not benefit from it, only Uncle Sam's ships can receive the accurate information; the rest of us must be content with a deliberately downgraded service. Unfortunately, Uncle Sam seems to vary the degree of downgrading without warning. We were at sea while Washington was celebrating the inauguration of a new President with a bit of aeronautical mayhem in Iraq. The GPS was off the air for several hours without any warning. You cannot grumble about this; it is a free service after all. But it means you cannot put 100% reliance on it. 99%, perhaps, but not 100%.

It seems to us, too, that one needs to know rather more than manufacturers care to reveal about the algorithm they use to convert the signals they receive into usable data form. Not that most of us could understand it (hands up those who know what an algorithm is for a start), but there are those who can, and equipment reviewers could give informed opinions on the relative merits of different brands. One could almost suppose that some 'user handbooks' are written to conceal rather than inform.

Mini-calculator navigation computer

Some people prefer to use one of these for the mathematical part of astro-navigation. It is handheld and runs on batteries (keep adequate spares in a waterproof container, and stick a little label on the calculator reminding you where they are), and is probably better for occasional use than a mass of tables. When astro-nav calculators first appeared on sale they had about twenty years of ephemera stored in them, to 1999. We notice that the models for sale now still have data to 1999 only, so you are getting rather less data for your money. Also the data they have is very limited; one we inspected had only basic tables for the sun and for the first point of Aries, which cuts out a lot of potentially useful sextant work. Those with only a few years' data stored ought to be on sale at a fraction of their original cost. It's time to do some bargaining.

Reliable alarm or four hour timer

A battery driven version of the kind that is sold in kitchenware departments is immensely useful, not only to remind you of change of watch, but of an upcoming sunsight, so easy to forget if the day is busy. As we get older we find anything that reminds us of these things to be of value. A problem could arise if you forget why you set the timer in the first place; see remarks under routine!

When you are choosing these gadgets, you will be doing us all a good turn if you express yourself forcefully to all salesmen, (and their bosses at the Boat Show if you are lucky) on the subject of buttons that are too small for us grownups to push, labels that are too small for us to read; and handbooks built on the model of the smallest Bible in the world. (Modern electronic devices are designed by people oblivious to the problems of adulthood, let alone old age.) Miniaturisation is one thing, but keypads, knobs and buttons should be of optimum ergonomic size. Many of these machines need to be used in times of stress and even danger, possibly in uncertain light; so buttons and keypads must be large and clearly labelled, and the handbook should be in large black print, and with a cover sturdy enough to cope with the inevitable coffee stains (though we hope never with sea water). Grey photocopies in fairy writing with floppy paper bindings are of no use to us, but the worst material of all is glossy paper pages which stick together permanently when within fifty miles of a drop of water, and the best handbook is no better than the worst if you cannot read it (keep a spare pair of glasses near the chart table *at all times*); it is still less use if it is so badly written as to be incomprehensible. While we are at it, we would like to discourage the use of designer hieroglyphs on the buttons and plugs of electronic devices. The laptop PC we are using at the moment has an output socket marked, apparently, with two plates and a knife and fork. It seems unlikely that we will get meals on wheels when we plug in. To sort this out, we bought little 'spot' labels in as many colours as possible, and use them in pairs, so that the red dot plug goes into the red dot socket. With complicated machines (including multi-voltage TV and radio) this is a great help in remembering what goes where. With all these machines you end up with interconnecting leads that are not always in use. Label them by wrapping a sticky label across the wire with a flap to write on, and put them in a sealable polythene bag, also labelled, or you end up (as we have done) with a bag of miscellaneous leads whose use has for the moment escaped us.

Radio receivers

These should have large clear dials or well-lit digitals (the latter are better) and big knobs, buttons, handwheels or levers. Sony made a very good SSB and short wave radio, the 2001, then they ruined it by reducing its size so that only fairy fingers can use the buttons. Radio direction finding is a thing of the past, but one needs a good radio with marine bands for weather forecasts, and the short wave to hear the BBC overseas service telling you the latest places not to visit.

All these electronic devices, of course, can go wrong, so there is still room for a little healthy distrust, and we suggest you do not commit yourself entirely to electronics unless you have two reliable back-up alternatives, not only to the individual pieces of equipment but also to the power supplies. Sextants need no electricity to run them, but are a little fiddly to use as you get older, so start off by understanding and familiarising yourself with them in good time.

Do your learning as early as you can: it would be of great benefit if you got your knowledge, whether on RYA courses or evening classes, even before you retire. It is much easier to go on doing something you are familiar with than gaining a whole new technical expertise in your 70's. There is nothing to prevent you learning as long as your brain cells continue to fire, but we are both very glad that at the age of 60 we did a computer course at the local evening classes while converting *Hosanna*: it stands us in good stead with modern equipment.

It is important not to keep your stand-by equipment at the back of the cupboard, never to see the light of day. Try to use it at regular intervals. Sextants, for example, are not wholly reliable until you are familiar with their use, and unless they have been kept lightly oiled. And it is all too easy to forget just where something you seldom use is stowed; the lead line for instance, which you might need at short notice. Writing that sentence produced a minor panic. Challenged, Bill could not produce the lead line. At least he *thought* he knew where it was; Laurel had no idea. He maintained that this put him one ahead in the preservation of faculties competition, but Laurel could not see the logic of this contention, her argument being that we were as bad as each other. It appears that we must have left it in *Fare Well* when we sold her, which shows how often we use it now, though in *Fare Well* we used it a lot.

Planning ahead

While the techniques you use to navigate may not change with advancing years, habits may have to. The most important thing in navigation was always in the area of care and planning, which one was sometimes tempted to skimp. Familiarity and relaxation gave a feeling that everything could be done on *an ad* hoc basis. That temptation should now be resisted. As one gets more forgetful, thorough preparation becomes vital, and the sooner it becomes a habit the better.

Whether you are singlehanded or not, it is important that for every voyage that is not already thoroughly familiar to you a proper plan is made in advance. Keep a special notebook for the purpose. Some instructors call this 'passage planning', but the word passage has a precise meaning, whereas the concept has a wider one.

Note in it the courses you expect to steer, the times you expect to reach various turning points or obstructions, with a 'bracket' to cover early and latest times.

Note down meteorological assumptions, and the times and radio frequency of weather forecasts you hope to hear. It is useful to record forecasts, so that you have time to replay and puzzle them out, some of them are done at machine-gun speed, and not in your native tongue. The BBC in particular like to employ readers from Glasgow, while the US Coast Guard recruit their readers from Dixie.

Note down the charts you will use, and the pages of the pilot books you might have to consult. Put cardboard markers in these pages. Draw 'highlight' circles round the important lighthouses and note their sighting range at your height of eye, which will be different from the figure printed on the chart.

In some parts of the world some terrible dangers are not marked, and on the old style of monochrome chart some that are marked do not stand out. Search for these odd dangers carefully and mark with a 'highlight' pen. When one needs reading glasses it is too easy to overlook something at night, say, with the lamp dimmed. Check that the colour of your highlighting survives poor light, or the red or other coloured lamps that many navigators use at night. In the old days all professional navigators constantly used magnifying glasses to read their charts, which had very small print. Some of the modern ones now have larger and clearer print (it is rumoured that new editions are going to have the words split into syllables with hyphens to help the illiterate), but there are still many old charts in the folios, and a careful perusal with a powerful magnifying glass is necessary. For example, the old symbol for a rock was a single tiny dot like a fly-speck: these were very difficult to pick out, and easy to overlook.

Note down any potential bolt-holes that you can run to in the event of rough weather, together with the limitations on their entry (eg 'do not enter in strong NE wind'). Note the whereabouts of places you can go to easily in case of accident.

Make a careful note of the dangers off-lying your destination, or any turning point, whether by day or night, good or bad visibility.

Religiously keep a position up to date on the chart, and revise the bolt-hole list as you go. Ships with radio operators always give the Wireless Office a latest position every four hours so that the operator can make an instant reply to a distress call. This sort of thing is professional. Set yourself a professional standard of prudence (even if you do not have a Wireless Office).

The reason behind all this, just in case we haven't made ourselves clear, is:

- To clarify your mind if you are singlehanded, when you may have other things to do at the same time.
- To assist your partner in the case where the skipper or navigator becomes unable to continue in harness. It is not likely to happen often, if at all, but your partner will be greatly aided if it does.
- To reduce the number of things you have to juggle with if something else goes wrong.

On our long voyages and ocean crossings Bill always logs the point at which it would no longer be reasonable to return, which is not necessarily the half-way mark. It is a good idea also to keep up to date a navigation policy for disaster. A chart in a waterproof envelope should be in the panic bag, and on very long voyages the position on this chart should be regularly updated too. This is more important if like us you do not carry a life-raft, but instead have a substantial weatherly, buoyant, half-decked sailing dinghy. Bill's view is that if the worst happened he would not be very happy sitting about bobbing up and down in a flimsy rubber liferaft surrounded by razor-sharp sharks' teeth, waiting to see if anyone turned up before we turned up our toes; he would rather shift himself horizontally to somewhere where we were more likely to find other craft, if not actually to cope on our own. He has a strong leaning towards coping on our own. He believes that should be the aim of all yachtsmen, and that we should not even think of bothering others to come to our assistance, other than in desperation or a real life-threatening disaster. And he has, after all, made an ocean passage in an open boat.

Much of the foregoing could be called a counsel of perfection. Clearly all that preparation is not needed for a sail across the estuary. But have a planning routine before setting sail, and keep to a minimum standard.

The philosophical navigator

Above all, maintain a frame of mind where time is not of the essence. Avoid arrival deadlines. Never meet aeroplanes. Tell your guests to book in at a hotel and enjoy themselves until you arrive, day unspecified. Never, ever, try to catch their plane for them. Make them travel to the airport, days ahead and by camel if necessary, leaving you happily and safely moored in a convenient and convivial spot. Try to keep alternatives open, and don't commit yourself to a chancy course to save time. Settle on a philosophy that it is better to spend a night lying hove-to at sea in some discomfort rather than trying to enter a tricky, unknown harbour in the dark. If it happens twice in your remaining lifetime we would be surprised, but it could be an important decision on the side of safety.

Those who would like some thought-provoking reading on the basics of non-electronic navigation might enjoy browsing through *Lecky's Wrinkles*. Written in the 1880s by a real old navigator in a wonderfully avuncular style, it contains a lot that is out of date, but it is in the oft-counselled attitude of mind that its value lies. All navigators in those days lived in fear; they were an extremely cautious class of people (the incautious did not survive). The attitude pervades his book, which was written by a man who spent a lifetime in the merchant service, and retired to look after his bees.

And would not those you might leave behind, as well as those who await you, be happier if they knew you were a really prudent mariner?

16

Come in, Number 9, Your Time is Up

There was an old woman who lived in a boat
It took three men with buckets to keep it afloat

YOUNG PEOPLE reading this will not remember that in our child-hood, when you hired a rowing boat for an hour on the lake, very few of us had watches; and those who did left them in the care of the boatman, since waterproof watches were owned only by millionaires who never had to hire a rowing boat. The boatman let you know when the hour had passed by calling out your number and telling you when your time was up.

If you are prevented from flying, it is known as being grounded, and can apply to planes or pilots. If you leave the sea and live ashore, old sailors called it swallowing the anchor.

Age concern

There may come a time when you both agree to leave your beloved boat and swallow the hook. Nothing wrong with that if it is your own decision, but beware of pressure from others to persuade you to do this (for your own good, of course) before you are quite ready.

You are:	They will say you are:
Firm	Obstinate
Resolute	Pigheaded
Steadfast	Stick in the mud
Reasonable	Unreasonable
Eccentric	Crackers
Self-sufficient	Selfish
Constant	Inflexible
Slowing down a bit	Doddery
Forgetful	Senile

Absentminded	Senile
Over seventy	Senile

and so on.

All it means is that *they* are beginning to worry about you, and want you somewhere where they can dissipate *their* worry in doing things for you that you do not want done.

It is hard to understand why people allow the young to risk death or injury with dangerous machines like motor bikes, and are loth to let the old have a similar privilege. It would make a lot more sense, really. We will have earned our old age when we get there, and should be able to spend it as we wish, even if our wishes do not suit everyone.

We have recently met a couple who had spent many happy years of living and cruising in a catamaran, and had been 'grounded' by their concerned relatives when they were in their mid-seventies. They had acquiesced for various reasons, and bought a villa on the Mediterranean coast. They did not make a preliminary visit to it in all seasons (see Chapter 6) and were horrified when the high summer came, to find themselves surrounded by hundreds of neighbours who whooped it up till the small hours, hogged the pool, and did not control the hordes of little ruffians who appeared to be their children. The couple are back in a boat again. Unfortunately they have made another mistake; not in going back to sea, but in buying a monohull due to their frantic haste to get away. 'It's not the right boat for us,' said the lady, aged 78. 'We're looking for another catamaran,' said her husband, aged 82.

Hands off the evening of our days. It isn't dark yet.

The final passage

All the same, one cannot be at sea in rough weather and not be acutely aware of one's mortality. Accidents can happen, and ships can sink. In fairness to those who love us and worry about us, we owe it to them to take every care, and let them know regularly that we are safe and well.

If the worst happens, it would be nice, from our own point of view, to go together. The one that's left from a lifelong partnership is always a sorry half-lived sort of thing for a while, even if they work through their grief and accept that everything has changed. In our case, the one surviving will have lost a way of life even if the boat survives, since we could neither of us do this alone. We are too accustomed to being a team.

So the survivor, or your children and/or executors, have the sad task of selling the boat or claiming the insurance, if any, just as they would have to sell your house and car and other belongings if you lived

'He says don't forget his entry for next year's
Whitbread.'

ashore. They are probably more at home with houses which are comparatively immobile. It would help everyone if you left behind you,
somewhere safe, a few documents.

- A will
- A detailed description and inventory of the boat, with a good pho-
  tograph, which would help a broker to sell it
- A list of bank accounts (surprising how many you might have,
  once you start thinking)
- A list of investments or savings
- What to do with your body, if it is available to do anything with

Here we should warn you that burial at sea is something you should
think very carefully about, however romantic it sounds. We could tell
some stories that counteract the heroic vision; the solemn weighty
slide of the coffin down the plank, slipping out from under the Union
Flag that shrouds it, and down to Davy Jones's locker. It is probably
the preferable option, as there is less to go wrong. The scattering of
ashes at sea is extremely fraught. The heart-rending photo of a wreath
tossing on the waves as often as not conceals the fact that the wind
changed at the critical moment, and the ashes of the beloved are being
brushed off the black clothes of the mourners. Casting the ashes inside
a nice heavy urn is not so aesthetic, but it is more practical, provided
the urn is heavy enough to sink. It also avoids a potential flurry of
feeding fish, which can be embarrassing.

The survivors, whether spouse, sons or daughters, will get little help
(in our experience) from consular offices abroad, and still less if you
were thoughtless enough to die on a Friday. The consulate golf is far
more important than the plight of your relatives, unless the deceased,
or one of his relatives, was rich, famous, or both. This was brought
home to us in Italy when a singlehander amongst us was killed in an
accident. The police stole his wallet at the scene; it contained phone
numbers that would have helped us a lot. It finally appeared that he
had no close relatives and his estranged wife was half a world away.
The consulate declined to help in any way whatsoever, even with
advice.

We, his fellow yachtsmen, organised his burial, and when the priest
turned up at the cemetery late and three sheets in the wind, we sent
him away and read the service ourselves from the *Ship Captain's
Medical Guide*. I think that is what the dead man might have preferred, since it was reverent and dignified, and he was among friends.

On another occasion a cruising friend of ours died, not on his boat,
but in a London hospital. Two bewildered maiden ladies arrived at his
boat's berth in the Mediterranean to settle his affairs. They knew

nothing about boats, and not a soul in the area. There were immense problems with local legislation. They were overwhelmed with sympathy, friendship, advice, and practical help, but none of it came from the consulate. It was the cruising people in boats close by who befriended them.

Notwithstanding what we said about sea burials, it has been known to be so difficult to land a body in some countries, what with the absence of ambulances, the understandable reluctance of taxis to carry corpses, the physical difficulties, and the red tape (authorities like you to die in the proper place, in hospital, where they have all the technology to cope with death as a matter of routine, but little of the warmth and sympathy you might get elsewhere) that it has sometimes led to the crew deciding to bury their shipmate at sea, rather than subject him to any further indignity. In many ways this is the best option. It is clean, dignified, and final.

There could be unexpected difficulties in dying in a devout but primitive Roman Catholic country where there is almost a superstitious attitude to burials. Some south and central American countries, for example, do not allow burial at sea, or even cremation, and make the export of bodies impracticable.

The authorities in almost all countries have surrounded the completely natural event of death with such a bewildering mass of regulations, none of which fit an unusual occasion, that an ordinary citizen finds it difficult to cope unaided. Our legislators ought to make it a bit easier to die with dignity, and a minimum of red tape with the black crape. Your surviving kin should be able to bury you or dispose of your remains according to your wishes (within reason and the limits of hygiene).

If someone dies in a port you will be bound by the laws of that country, but if he should die at sea, you have considerably more freedom. We will tell you enough to help a survivor make a decision that will ease *their* problems. He who has died no longer has any.

The legal position on burial at sea is contained in The Merchant Shipping (Returns of Births and Deaths) Regulations 1979.

1 Be certain that the person is dead and not comatose after head injury, or torpid following hypothermia, to take just two possible examples. If there is more than one of you to agree about this, so much the better. Facts and times should be entered in the log and signed by all present. Even if there is an area of disagreement, both views should be recorded; frankness is everything. If the person is lost at sea, the same applies.

2 The Master of a ship is required to make a return of deaths in or from a ship. It must be made as soon as practicable (but cer-

tainly within six months) to either a Marine Superintendent in the UK, a British Consular Office in foreign countries, or the equivalent of a Marine Superintendent in a Commonwealth country. The Regulations warn that there will be local regulations and procedures to be satisfied if the body is landed at a port, but the UK regulations apply whether or not the body is landed, buried at sea, or not recovered.

The legal record of the death is in the register entry made by the Registrar following the report of the Master of the ship.

3   The burial should take place in deep water, preferably out of soundings (more than 100 fathoms).
4   A strong shroud in the form of a bag is desirable, with slits in it.
5   You should record in the log the time and place of burial, and get countersignatures if you can.
6   While on the high seas a British registered ship is considered to be within British legal jurisdiction, but once she enters the waters of another country the situation is not clear, particularly if citizens of that country are involved.

If the bureaucracy of one country can be considered indecently oppressive, just think of trying to cope with two or more. Betty tells the story of a death on a charter holiday of a young American. His mother was in Mexico, the yacht was British; the charter had been organised by a French company and the death occurred in Monte Carlo. The passengers and crew were forbidden to leave the yacht for three weeks, which was the time it took five countries to sort it all out.

In many cases involving old folk while cruising, it is likely there will be only two persons on board. In these circumstances it is arguably justified that the survivor should see that any obsequies are carried out to the complete satisfaction of the two of them alone. Put the registration details in the post as and when you wish during the next six months, and then go into a condition of grief and selective shock which would enable you to exclude all consideration of anything else to do with the event that you feel unable to cope with. At your age, and in your circumstances, no one will be in any position to harass you.

For further information we refer you to the excellent chapter on the dying and the dead in *The Ship Captain's Medical Guide.*

If your relations with your descendants merit it, then we feel that it is no bad thing to have a discussion of the points we raise while the problem is still theoretical. If everyone is aware of the difficulties, then if the awful event does happen, there should be a better understanding.

Sunset and evening star
And one clear call for me!
And may there be no moaning at the bar
When I put out to sea

Alfred, Lord Tennyson

When the twilight comes, and we really are too old to go to sea, not just a danger to ourselves (we *must* be allowed to be that) but a serious danger to others and the rescue services, then call us in gently, and try to understand our feelings. We shall probably know ourselves when it is time for Number 9 to come in.

EPILOGUE

We have had to face some hard facts in writing this book, both on our own behalf and in trying to wear the shoes of others. It has been at times a disconcerting and salutary experience. We have had to be very honest about our limitations, and ask ourselves some questions that we might have preferred to ignore. If we could know what is to come, there would be no such thing as optimism, so it is just as well that the gods veil our future, and allow us to live in hope. We have watched with aching sympathy while old friends gave up sailing because of ill-health, or lack of enthusiasm in themselves or their partners. We have observed with passionate interest the shift of the newly retired (usually prodded by their wives) to dryer, steadier, and more comfortable craft, from tidal waters to quiet canals, from small dinghies to larger boats, or vice versa, whatever was needed to keep them afloat.

All very well dreaming in an armchair, our critics might say, how wonderful, how comfortingly appropriate to grey hairs; that will keep them off the streets. But if you really want to do it, reality, they say, must break in at some point. Such critics could do with a gentle beating round the head with a zimmer frame. At our age, we are always balancing on the borders of what is possible.

It follows that we have encouraged those who wanted our advice on sailing to ask themselves hard questions and to go for it if the answers seem reasonable. Reality, we are glad to say, is alive and well and living on the water to a great age.

Reality is 'les trois granies', Liz, Helen and Gill, cruising northern France in *La Snook* (7.25 metres), bearing lightly their combined 222 summers.

Reality is the numberless white-haired couples we have met, happily cruising in home waters or distant places, some in sailing boats, some in canal cruisers, some in boats that we should not dare to recommend, but which they manage with an efficiency born of long familiarity.

Reality is the old French gentleman we saw on what seemed to be a water bicycle, who was so charmed by the plaudits of the watching crowd that he failed to notice an approaching low ·bridge over the

Les Trois Granies. *This photo, which first appeared in the French newspaper* Ouest France, *is of three splendid English ladies, Liz, Helen and Gill, with a combined age of 222 years, who cruise each year in the 7.25 m yacht* La Snook. *Their voyage into the difficult waters off Brittany caught the imagination of the French, and we share their feelings of admiration. What strikes us as odd is that passers-by, seeing the yacht with its three ladies, assume there is a man on board somewhere to do all the work. Why?*

canal and had to fall off into the water to avoid a bang on his ancient pate.

Reality is old salts alone, perfectly happy, performing feats of voyaging that leave their youngers breathless, and cause the heart attacks among their kin that they are themselves avoiding.

Reality is Lady Mayhew racing *Pochard* in her eighties.

Reality is our American buddies in *Snow Goose*, caught on the Intracoastal Waterway in hurricane Hugo, retaining enough presence of mind to relay vital meteorological data to the authorities via their 'ham' radio.

Fortunately for us, real life on the water includes a vast navy of splendid old sailors, in craft of every kind, large and small, sail, motor, and bicycle wheels, suitable and unsuitable.

Long, very long, may it be so.

Appendix 1

Initial Stability of Boats

Figures 4 and 5 on pages 188–189 should be looked at together. They represent cross-sections of two types of boat: 4A, 4B, and 4C show a boat, *Onesie,* with high initial stability, and 5A, 5B, and 5C show a boat, *Twosie,* with low initial stability. The suffixes A, B, and C show each boat in similar situations: A when they are floating normally, B when they have been heeled over a few degrees, and C in rather dire straits when heeled over to ninety degrees.

Both 4A and 5A show the boats safely floating. The letter G represents the centre of gravity, and the weight of the boats acts directly downwards through this point no matter how they are heeled. The letter B shows in all cases the centre of buoyancy, which is effectively the centre of the cross sectional area of the hulls below the waterline. The weight of the boat in each case equals the buoyancy. The force of buoyancy acts straight upwards through the centres of buoyancy.

The centres of gravity are always in the same places within each boat, no matter how they are heeled, but the centres of buoyancy move sideways as the boats start to heel and the shapes of the immersed parts of the boats start to change. In 4B notice that the relative positions of the lines of the two forces of weight and buoyancy have moved apart by the distance Y, and that this is considerably more than X, the distance of the two lines of force in 5B.

The righting moment, which is the force that returns the boat to its stable upright condition, is the weight of the boat multiplied by the distance Y or X as appropriate for the particular boat. This righting moment can be plotted against angle of heel to give the stability curve of an individual boat.

To round off the picture, 4C and 5C show an extreme condition. Note that now the situation is not so good for *Onesie.* Her centre of buoyancy has moved back until it is virtually under the centre of gravity. There is almost no righting moment at all. She is in real trouble. On the other hand *Twosie,* which, at a small angle of heel had a small righting moment, and thus poor initial stability, now looks much the more healthy. The centre of gravity, which her lead keel brings well down into the boat, is now well separated from the centre of buoyancy, and she has a very healthy righting moment, and will bounce back upright.

Generally speaking, you do not have high initial stability with high ultimate stability. The high ultimate stability is usually only needed in extreme conditions when pushing a boat to the very limit. Mostly boats remain at low angle of heel, and this is where steadiness is needed.

We suggest that for older persons, a boat having a cross-section shaped somewhere nearer *Onesie* than *Twosie* would be safer, more comfortable, and more easily managed.

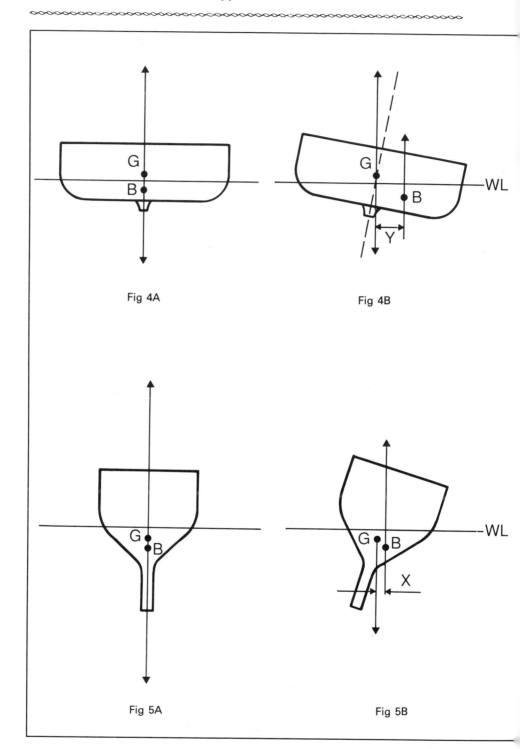

Fig 4A

Fig 4B

Fig 5A

Fig 5B

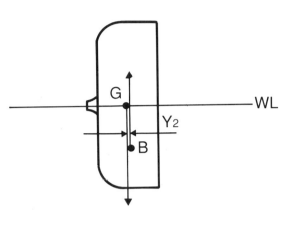

Fic 4C

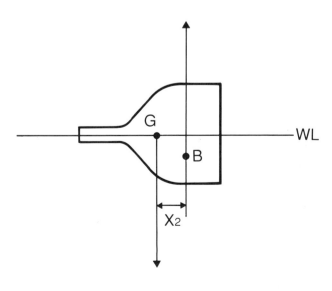

Fig 5C

Appendix 2

ᗡᗡᗡᗡᗡᗡᗡᗡᗡ

French Canal Dues

We give below some information on this subject, translated and paraphrased from a document entitled *Information to Pleasure Boat Users on Navigable Waterways*, dated 10 Dec 1991 and signed by Jean Chapon, President of Voies Navigables de France (VNF). Obviously the original regulations in French are paramount in the case of any misunderstanding; our summary in translation has no legal force whatsoever.

The tax is due on all boats of more than 5 metres in length, or with a motor of more than 9.9 hp. (This presumably applies to French legal horse power, which is an artificial conception which, for example, can rate a well-known motor car at 2 hp).

It must be paid in advance no matter how short the voyage.

The tariff is based on the square metreage of the surface area occupied by the vessel.

The surface area is calculated by the length overall, ignoring balconies, and diverse apparatus, multiplied by the overall beam.

The toll does not include any mooring rights, and any long-term mooring outside approved ports must be the subject of a special authorisation.

Anyone navigating without displaying a *vignette* will be liable to the most awful penalties.

Rates for 1992/3:

Annual	50FF/sq m
Season 15/5 to 31/10	30FF/sq m
Monthly	20FF/sq m
Weekly	5FF/sq m
Daily	1FF/sq m

TVA (VAT to us) is not payable on the dues. We hear that for 1994 some changes are likely.

Application by post or in person to the Bureaux d'Affrètement at the following towns: Arles, Bethune, Bordeaux, Calais, Chalons-sur-Saône, Compiègne, Conflans St Honorine, Douai, Dunkerque, Le

Havre, Lille, Lyon, Marseille, Mulhouse, Nancy, Paris, Reims, Rouen, St Jean-de-Losne, St Mammes, St Quentin, Sarreguemines, Sète, Strasbourg, Thionville, Toulouse, Valenciennes, Vitry-le-Francois.

Payment can also be made at the head office of VNF, but only by post: Monsieur l'Agent Comptable, 2 Boulevard Latour Maubourg 75007, Paris. Tel 49 55 60 00.

All applications by post must have a stamped addressed envelope, and contain payment in French francs. You will receive your vignette by post. Note that no concessions or alternative arrangements have been made for persons abroad.

Appendix 3

Some Useful Addresses

Laying up
The best we know, with a high standard, is Joe Charlton's company, Contract Yacht Services Ltd, of Petrou Filippa 3A, Levkas 31100, Greece, Tel 0645 24490. He will not take on more than he can manage properly, and in consequence he has a waiting list.

Books on canals
For anyone interested in reading about canals, Hugh McKnight has an excellent mail-order bookshop specialising in new, out of print, or antique books about inland waters the world over. Address: Shepperton Swan, The Clock House, Upper Halliford, Shepperton, Middx, TW17 8RU.

Builders of penichettes
Locaboat Plaisance
Port au Bois, 89300 Joigny, France. Tel 89 91 72 72.
Fax France 86 62 42 41.

Dutch Barge Association
Those interested in barging may like to know of this association. There are 700 Dutch barges in British private ownership and the association is an excellent source of information, with a quarterly magazine. Address: Bossington Wharf, Linslade, Leighton Buzzard, Beds, LU7 7TF

Barge Agents
Friesland Boating, Koudum, Holland. Tel 5142 2607, Fax 5142 2620.
H2O, St Jean-de-Losne, France. Tel 80 39 23 00, Fax 80 39 04 67.
Living on Water, Amsterdam, Holland. Tel 2038 1988, Fax 2020 2200.

MASTA Medical Advisory Services for Travellers Abroad
Bureau of Hygiene and Tropical Diseases, Keppel Street, London
WC1E 7 HT
Tel 071-636 8636.

INDEX